HISTORY OF EGYPT

BY

F. C. H. WENDEL, A. M., Ph. D.

ISBN: 978-1-63923-953-5

Printed: March 2023

Published and Distributed By:
Lushena Books
607 Country Club Drive, Unit E
Bensenville, IL 60106
www.lushenabks.com

ISBN: 978-1-63923-953-5

PREFACE.

In presenting to the public this little book, which treats of the history of ancient Egypt from the earliest times to the conquest by Alexander the Great, my object has been twofold: First, to give to American readers a brief account of Egyptian history which would be as reliable as the present state of Egyptological science permits; and, second, to create a deeper interest in the study of ancient Egypt. The study of Egyptology is of the greatest importance to the theologist, the historian, the student of civilization, and the art-student. In science and art Egypt was the teacher of Greece; even the Greek alphabet is derived from the Egyptian through the medium of the Phœnician, and Greece was the teacher of Europe.

The basis of a rational study of Egyptology will always be a thorough knowledge of Egyptian history; without this the student can not properly understand the development of Egypt's civilization—of its science, its religion, its art, its language, and its literature. I have in the following pages given as complete a history as the space allotted would permit. In the introductory chapter I have not been able to give as much space as I should have wished to the subjects there treated, and have been compelled to confine myself to what was absolutely necessary. Science, art, and literature could not be treated, as even a partial account of them would have required too much space.

In regard to the sources of my book, I have, as a rule,

confined myself to the Egyptian monuments, using foreign sources only in emergencies, where no native sources are extant for the period in question. It may appear strange to some readers that I have not treated of the Exodus. This event does not, however, properly belong to Egyptian history. It did not at all affect Egypt, however important it may have been to the Israelites.

In my chronology I have followed Eduard Meyer, the famous German historian, who introduced a system of so-called "approximate dates," which are always the *latest* dates that can be given for an era. Thus, when we say that King Mena ruled about 3200 B. C., that King Snefru ruled about 2830 B. C., and Pepi I, 2530 B. C., we would not by any means imply that these dates are absolutely correct; but we would merely imply that these monarchs could not have ruled *after* the dates given, though we can not say how long *before* these dates they did live. Snefru may even have ruled five hundred years before 2830 B. C., but we have no means of knowing his exact date. From the date of Aahmes I's accession to the throne, about 1530 B. C., Meyer's dates are approximately correct. We *know* that King Necho ruled 609–595 B. C., that Sheshong I lived about 930 B. C., that Ramses II lived in the thirteenth and Thutmosis III in the fifteenth century B. C., but we know, as an absolute certainty, nothing more. These approximate dates are, however, such a convenience that it would be well to adopt them until we can give the exact dates. The maps here given have been most carefully prepared, and will, I hope, greatly assist the reader in understanding the history of the great campaigns.

With these few prefatory remarks I submit this booklet to the judgment of the public, and, if I succeed in the twofold object of spreading the truth so far as discoverable, and creating a deeper interest in ancient Egypt, I shall rest content.

F. C. H. WENDEL, A. M., PH. D.

NEW YORK CITY, *November* 11, 1889.

CONTENTS.

MAPS.

HISTORY OF EGYPT.

CHAPTER I.

INTRODUCTORY.

§ 1. *The Ancient Geography of Egypt.*

EGYPT lies in the northeastern corner of Africa, between the twenty-fourth and the thirty-second degrees of
north latitude. It is bounded on the east by Asia and the
Red Sea, on the south by a line drawn east and west
through Assuan, on the First Cataract, on the west by
the Desert of Sahara, and on the north by the Mediterranean Sea. This tract of country is five hundred and
twenty miles long, and on an average one hundred and sixty
miles wide. The area of the entire country is about one
hundred thousand square miles, or about two and a half
times that of Ohio. But the whole of this country is not
cultivable ; by far the larger part is desert—on the west a
low, arid, sandy plain ; on the east an arid mountain region. Only the immediate valley of the Nile is arable soil,
and this is a very narrow strip, which between Assuan
and the Delta never exceeds fifteen miles in width, and at
places is only two miles wide. In the Delta there is a far
wider stretch of cultivable land, owing to the fact that
the Nile here divides into numerous branches ; but even
here all the land is not available for cultivation, owing
to numerous great swamps and large lakes. In antiquity the greater part of the Delta was swamp and
meadow land ; and its chief value lay in the fact that it
was a good grazing country, and that its swamps and
lakes made fine hunting-grounds, abounding as they did
in all sorts of aquatic birds. The lakes were full of fish,
so that fishing was added to grazing and hunting, and
thus the country possessed considerable resources even
before agriculture became profitable. It is well known

that Egypt owes this strip of good land to the Nile. This remarkable river, which rises in the Nyanza Lakes in tropical Africa, and has several branches which come from the Ethiopic highlands, is annually swollen by the rains which prevail in the tropics during the rainy season. Already in June the river begins to rise, and continues to swell until about September 15th, when it reaches the high-water mark. It then remains stationary until late in October, when it begins to fall, and by January the river is again at its old level. So important was this rise of the Nile to the entire population, that the ancient Egyptians made the day on which the river attained its highest level, September 15th. their New-year's-day (called in Egyptian *up rompet*). The inundation brought coolness, humidity, and fertility. The river brought down from the Ethiopian highlands vast masses of mud, which it deposited on the Egyptian soil when it inundated the land, and which remained there when the water receded. Thus an alluvial soil of great depth and richness was produced. The full benefits of the inundation could not, however, be gained without hard work on the part of the dwellers in the Nile valley. As rain was in antiquity almost entirely wanting in Egypt, a carefully arranged system of irrigation was necessary to convey the much-needed moisture to the more remote fields. The digging of canals from the river and building of reservoirs were not easy work; and, moreover, the overflow had to be carefully regulated in accordance with the character of the various fields, should the full results be obtained. Thus we see that the Egyptian farmer could not sit with folded arms and let his generous river do the work for him. He had to be up and doing from early morning till late at night, to reap the full benefits obtainable from his wonderful stream.

Before we touch the old geographical division of the country, we may well say a few words of the character of the rocky highlands that fringe the Nile valley. At the First Cataract the river breaks through a vast granite barrier that here crosses the Nubian sandstone deposit. At this place the Egyptians had established, already in the times of King Chufu (about 2800 B. C.), great quarries from which they took their supply of granite. In the same neighborhood basalt, too, was quarried about this time. The Nubian sandstone then continues as far north as

Silsileh, where the Egyptians early worked sandstone quarries. The character of the hills now changes, a little to the north of Silsileh, the sandstone giving place to a tertiary nummulitic limestone, which formation continues on both sides of the Nile, on the west to the Mediterranean, on the east to Memphis, whence it strikes off to the northeast. These rocky hills seldom reach and never exceed the moderate height of six hundred to eight hundred feet. The character of the mountain region between the Nile and the Red Sea is, however, vastly different. Here we meet with grand and imposing mountain scenery, the bold, many-colored mountain-peaks often reaching a height of six thousand feet. These mountains consist of crystalline rock, granite, gneiss, porphyry, diorite, and others. Several valleys lead from the Nile into this region. The most important of these is the Wâdi Hammamât, the *Rohanu* of the ancient Egyptians, a valley extending from Qeneh on the Nile to Qosêr, on the Red Sea. This valley was used in antiquity as a trade route between the Nile valley and the sea, the point of departure being in olden times the city of *Qebti* (the Koptos of the Greeks, the modern Quft), and the Red Sea port being some place near the modern Qosêr). For a time it was at the extremity of the Wâdi Gasûs, north of Qosêr. This valley had in antiquity a further significance. Midway between the Nile and the Red Sea the Egyptians worked in very early times diorite quarries of considerable extent.

So much for the general character of the land. We now turn to a consideration of the ancient geography. The Egyptian official name of the state was *Taui*, " both lands "—i. e., both North and South Egypt ; the name *Qemet*, " the black (land) " was also often used, though not in state documents. From this name was derived the Coptic name of the country, KHME in Sahidic, XHMI in Boheiric, from which latter form was derived the Hebrew *Ham* (הָם). The country was divided into two parts, the South, known in Egyptian as *Rês* or *Qemat*, " the South," and as *Pa ta rês*, " the South Land," which latter name gave rise to the Hebrew *Patrôs*, the Παθούρης of the Septuaginta, and the North, designated in the Egyptian as *Mehta* " the North," and *Pa ta mera*. The " South " included all the land from Assuan to Memphis, the " North " all of the Delta. Why this division was made we shall see in § 3. Each

of these countries was divided into a number of small districts, which we are accustomed to designate as *nomes*,
generally given as forty-two in number, twenty-two in
Upper and twenty in Lower Egypt. I here enumerate
the twenty-two Upper Egyptian and the principal Lower
Egyptian nomes, going from south to north, and stating
as briefly as possible what interest attaches to each: I.
The southernmost nome, *Ta Chont*, extended from Assuan
to Silsileh. Its chief town was the city of *Abu* (Greek Ele-
phantinê), situated on an island in the Nile. Opposite this
city, on the river-bank, lay the town of *Swen*, where the old
granite quarries were situated; *Swen* became in Greek
Syene, and from this, by prefixing the article, the Arabs
made *As·suan*. On the northern boundary of the nome
lay the sandstone quarries of Silsileh. The deity worshiped in this nome was the god *Chnum*. II. The second nome was called *Tes Hor*. Its capital and religious
center was the famous old town of *Debhot*, the modern
Edfu, where the well-preserved ruins of the temple erected
by the Ptolemies to the local divinity *Hor Debehti*, a form
of the god Horus still excite the admiration of the beholder.
III. The third nome, *Ten*, with the capital *Nechebet*, the
modern *Elkab*, Greek *Eletheia*, the home of the old tutelar
deity of Upper Egypt, the goddess *Nechebet*, had for local
deity the god *Chnum*. Two other cities of importance
were situated in this nome: *Enyt*, the modern *Esneh*,
where there stands a fairly preserved temple built in Ptolemaic times, and the city of *On*, called "*On* of the god
Mont," in contradistinction to *On - Heliopolis*, the city
of Râ, in Lower Egypt; it is the Greek *Hermonthis*, and
Arabic *Erment*. IV. Now follows the fourth nome, *Oueset*, the capital of which was the famous city of *Oueset*
(commonly known by its Greek name *Thebes*); its chief
divinity was *Amon*; *Mentu* was worshiped in the southern portion. V. *Horui*, the capital of which was the city
of *Qebti*, situated on the Nile at the entrance to the Wâdi
Hammamât, of which we have spoken above; the local
divinity was the god *Min*. VI. *Aati* had chiefly religious
importance; its capital, *Ta ent terer* (modern *Denderah*,
Greek *Tentyris*), was the home of the great goddess *Hathor*. Her temple, built by the Ptolemies, is fairly preserved. VII. The nome *Sechem*, the capital of which was
Hat (*Diospolis parva*) had the same local divinity, *Hathor*.

VIII. *Abt* was one of the most important nomes; its capital was *Abdu* (*Abydos*) the seat of the *Osiris* religion, and alleged burial-place of the god. IX. The ninth nome, *Min*, with the capital *Per-Min* (House of Min), Greek *Panopolis*, had but little importance. X. This nome, called *Ouatjet*, the capital of which was *Debu* (*Aphroditopolis*), worshiped the goddess *Hathor ;* the district *Neterui*, with the capital *Duqa* and the god *Horus*, formed part of it. XI. The eleventh nome, *Set*, the capital of which was *Shas-hotep* (*Hypsele*), was devoted to the god *Chnum*. XII. *Duhefu* had as capital the town of *Nut ent Bek* and worshiped the god *Horus*. The chief importance of this nome lay in its valuable alabaster quarries, which were worked in very early times, near the ancient city of *Hat-nub*, the modern *Ebnub*. XIII. The nome *Atefchont*, the capital of which was the old city of *Saiut* (*Siut*), a town that in the Middle Empire (2100–1900 B. C.), was of considerable importance, owing to the influential and powerful position occupied by its nomarchoi; it was the chief seat of the cult of the jackal-headed god of the Dead *Anubis*. XIV. *Atefpeh* was unimportant ; its capital was *Qesi* (*Cusæ*), and its deity *Hathor*. XV. The nome of *Ouen* had for capital the city of *Chmunu* (Greek *Hermopolis*, modern *Eshmunên*), which derived its name from the fact that it was the seat of the eight gods of the elements, so called ; the chief divinity of the nome was the god of wisdom *Thot*. XVI. *Mehmahet* was of great importance in the times of the Middle Empire, owing to its influential and mighty nomarchoi, whose tombs were discovered at Benihassan. To these tombs, which are hewn into the living rock, and the walls of which are covered with important representations and inscriptions, we owe much of what we know of this period. The capital was *Hebenu*, and the local divinity *Horus*. XVII. The capital of the nome *Anbu* was *Kasa* (*Cynonpolis*) ; its god was *Anubis*. XVIII. *Sapet*, the capital of which was *Hatbenu* (*Alabastronpolis*), one of the seats of the *Anubis* cult, was important for its alabaster quarries, which were opened in early times. XIX. *Ouab*, the capital of which was the city of *Permatjet* (*Oxyrrhynchos*), was the only nome where *Set* was worshiped. From this nome led the roads to the oases of the eastern Sahara. XX. This nome bore the name *Atefchont*. Its capital was

2

Chenensuten (Heracleopolis magna), a city of great importance in the religion of Egypt, as the god *Rā* was supposed to have made his first appearance here. The local divinity of the nome was *Horshāfi*, a form of Horus. XXI. *Atefpeh* had for capital the city of *Semenhor*, and for local deity the god *Chnum*. The western part was know as *Ta-she*, "Lakeland," the modern name of the region being *Fayoum*, which is derived from the ancient word *Pa-yôm*, "the sea," through the medium of the Boheiric dialect of the Coptic, in which it became *Pha-yôm*. Here was situated the great reservoir built by Amenhotep III. XXII. The northernmost nome of Upper Egypt was known as *Māten*. Its capital was *Tepah*, and its local deity the goddess *Hathor*.

Of the twenty Lower Egyptian nomes I shall enumerate only the principal ones : I. *Anbu-hetj*, the nome of *Mennefer (Memphis)*, the city of *Ptah*. IV. *Sepi-res*, the nome of *Tjeka (Canopus)*, where *Amon-Rā* was worshiped. V. *Sepi-em-het*, the nome of *Sa (Saïs)*, where the great goddess *Neit* was worshiped, the home of the Psametichs. IX. *Atji*, the nome of *Per-Usiri (Busiris)*, the city of *Osiris*. XII. *Katjeb*, the nome of *Tjebneter (Sebennythos)*, the home of the god *Anhur*. XIII. *Hakad*, the nome of *On (Heliopolis)*, the great seat of the *Rā* religion. XIV. *Chentabed*, the nome of *Tjan (Tanis)*, where *Horus* was worshiped. XVI. *Char*, the nome of *Per-Banebded (Mendes)*, the god of which was the sacred ram *Banebded*. XVIII. *Amchent*, the nome of *Per-bastet (Bubastis)*, the city of the cat-headed goddess *Bastet*. XIX. *Ampeh*, the name of *Per-Ouatj (Buto)*, where *Ouatj*, the tutelar deity of Lower Egypt, had her home.

§ 2. *The Sources of Egyptian History.*

It is needful in a history of Egypt to give a brief summary of the sources from which our knowledge of the facts is derived. These sources are : *a. National; b. Asiatic ;* and *c. Classical.*

a. National Sources.—Before we give any account of the monuments and documents on which by far the greatest part of Egyptian history is based, it may be well to review rapidly the history of the decipherment of the hieroglyphics and to give a brief sketch of the Egyption system of writing.

Already in the Middle Ages men like Athanasius Kircher attempted to decipher the "mysterious picture-writing" of ancient Egypt; but their interpretations, proceeding from an utter misconception of the true nature of the hieroglyphics, were fantastical and utterly useless. The results attained by these men discredited the study of hieroglyphics, and scholars turned rather to Coptic, the liturgic language of the Christian Church of Egypt, a descendant of the Egyptian tongue, and at the time still a living language. The results attained in this study were later on of great value to the decipherers of the ancient tongue. In August, 1799, there was unearthed at Rosetta a block of black basalt bearing a decree of Ptolemy Epiphanes in Greek, hieroglyphics, and demotic—the celebrated "*Rosetta stone.*" Immediately scholars set to work at deciphering the inscription. *Thomas Young*, an English mathematician, and *François Champollion*, a French *savant*, working independently of one another, succeeded at about the same time in deciphering the royal names in the hieroglyphical part, and, to the surprise of all, it was found that the writing was largely phonetic. Champollion's results were by far the more important, and when, ten years after his first great discovery, he died in 1832, he had already correctly given the contents of entire inscriptions and papyri, and had laid down the elements of a grammar. Ten years later *Richard Karl Lepsius*, the great German Egyptologist, who died some years ago, carried further the work so ably begun by Champollion, and through him the final proof was given that the results so far attained were correct. He discovered in 1867 at Tanis a trilingual inscription—the so-called "*Decree of Canopus*"—the study of which document finally confirmed the results hitherto obtained from the study of the Egyptian texts. Thus the stage of decipherment came to a close. Since then able scholars in all parts of Europe have been adding to our knowledge of Egyptian matters.

The Egyptian system of writing appears at first glance to be highly complicated, but it is in reality far simpler than it looks. It is a combination of the *phonetic—alphabetic* and *syllabic* — and *ideographic* systems, to

which is added a system of *determinatives.* The alphabet consists of twenty-two *consonants*—vowels are, as in
all other old Semitic languages, not written. The alphabetic and syllabic signs are by far the oldest, the most
ancient texts being purely phonetic, containing neither
ideograms nor determinatives. Owing to the fact that
the vowels were not written, confusion early arose among
words having the same consonants but different significa-
tions, and, in all probability, pronounced with different
vowels. To obviate this difficulty, the Egyptians early
invented a system of *determinatives.* A determinative is
the picture of an object placed *after* the word signifying
the object in question. Determinatives are either *generic*
or *specific.* The *generic determinative* is the picture of
some object which is characteristic of a group. Thus,
after the names of animals we frequently find the picture
of a piece of skin ; after abstract words and verbs we find
the picture of a papyrus roll ; and after the names of foreign countries we find the picture of a range of hills. The
specific determinative is the picture of the object that the
word denotes. Thus, after the word *hetra*, signifying
"horse," the picture of a horse was often placed ; after
the word *abu*, denoting "panther," we often find a picture
of that animal ; after the word *romet*, "man," we find the
picture of a man, as also after the names of males ; after
the word *suten*, "king," we find the picture of a king ;
after the word *himet*, "woman," the names of females
and goddesses, we find the picture of a woman ; and after
the names of cities we find the plan of a city. From these
determinatives arose in course of time *ideograms*, or
word-pictures. Thus the plan of a city, originally the
determinative of the word *nut*, "city," came with time to
stand for the word itself, which is never written phonetic-
ally ; the picture of a bee, originally the determinative of
the word *afet*, "honey," came with time to be used as the
ideogram for that word ; the figure of a man walking with
a long staff, originally the determinative of the word *ser*,
"prince," later on was used as an ideogram. Many other
examples could be given, but these will illustrate the general
principle. In Ptolemaic times the ideograms were greatly
multiplied, many texts being written almost entirely in ideograms. It must, however, always be borne in mind that
the writing was originally *phonetic*, and not *ideographic.*

The writing, too, has a history of its own. In the oldest times the writing was purely *hieroglyphical.* Hiero-glyphics were written as early as 4000 B. C., if not earlier, and continued in use far into the times of the Roman em-perors. These hieroglyphics were originally finely exe-cuted in every detail, and this remained the custom on all government monuments so long as hieroglyphics were used. But it was early found that the full hieroglyphics, while admirably adapted for inscriptions on stone, were too cumbersome for writing on papyrus or mummy-bands (which were of linen), so an abridged or cursive form, that we call *linear hieroglyphics*, was invented. These linear hieroglyphics are merely the characteristic outlines of the full signs. They remained in use all through Egyptian history for religious texts written on papyrus and mummy-bands. About 1700 B. C. a new method of writing came into vogue for profane writings. This new method, which still further abridged the hieroglyphics, is called *Hieratic.* The *older form* of this hieratic still in some measure resembles the linear hieroglyphical writing from which it was derived. Some four hundred years this method seems to have been in use, when a *new system* came into being, which is also called *hieratic*, but differs materially from the older style, from which it is abridged, in that it is far less cumbersome, omitting many of the details found in the older hieratic, and being thus far more suitable for rapid writing. From this *newer hie-ratic* was derived the *Phœnician* alphabet, from which the Greek alphabet was derived. This form of the hieratic is thus the ancestor of our alphabet. This style of writing remained in fashion many hundred years as the cursive script used on papyrus, and sometimes even on mummy-bands. The last stage in the development of Egyptian script was reached in the *Demotic* in the fifth century be-fore the Christian era. This was a still further abridg-ment of the new hieratic, but it eliminated so many details that very many letters and syllabic signs that had been kept distinct in hieratic became one and the same sign, a fact that renders the reading of Demotic very difficult. The new system had, however, the advantage of being very rapid, and thus it quickly supplanted the hieratic ; it remained in use up to the Christian times, when it was supplanted by the Coptic script, which was modeled after the Greek. The reader must not, however, imagine that these changes were sudden; one led gradually to the other. Thus the old, full hieroglyphics were abridged in the linear hieroglyphics, from these was developed the old hieratic, from this the new hieratic, and this, becoming gradually more and more cursive, led over to the Demotic.

We now pass to a consideration of the Egyptian sources from which our knowledge of the facts of Egyptian history is derived. The texts which are of primary importance are the lists of kings compiled in antiquity. The most important of these is the so-called " *Turin Papyrus of Kings*," which gives a list of Egyptian kings from the earliest times to the times of the sixteenth dynasty (about 1700 B. C.), including the earlier kings of this dynasty, in which it was most probably written. This list is chronological, the duration of the reign of each king in years, months, and days, being given after his name. Unfortunately, however, the papyrus is fragmentary, having been broken into one hundred and sixty-four small pieces on the way to Turin. Prof. Seyffarth conferred a lasting benefit on historical science by arranging, numbering, and mounting these fragments, thus preserving this valuable document. The second list of importance is that discovered in the temple of Osiris in Abydos. This list contains the names of seventy-five predecessors of Seti I (about 1320 B. C.), arranged in chronological order. The third list was discovered in a private tomb dating from the times of Ramses II (1300 to 1230 B. C.); it enumerates forty-seven kings. The last important list is that found in Karnak, which enumerates sixty-one predecessors of Thutmosis III (1480 to 1430). Besides these a number of smaller and less important lists have been discovered. Next in importance to the lists stand the *official inscriptions* of the kings. The pharaohs were in the habit of inscribing on the walls of the temples they erected to the gods long accounts of their deeds. In order to be able to give a full account of their campaigns the kings were accompanied by scribes specially detailed to write down the history of these campaigns. Their accounts were then copied on the temple walls. Great paintings illustrating the principal events of a campaign covered the space not occupied by the inscriptions, in that part of the temple allotted to the annals. These inscriptions were divided into two parts—the date, on which followed, as a rule, a laudatory hymn to the king, and the account of the campaign. These texts give a chronological account of the campaigns of the king, often going into the details of the march and of the various battles. Among the most interesting of these inscriptions is a copy of the treaty of peace and alliance between Ramses II and Chetasar, king of the Cheta, which was originally engraved on a silver plate, and from this was copied on the outer wall of the temple of Karnak, where it has been completely preserved. Of importance are further royal decrees, which are frequently found inscribed on stelæ and temple walls. Reports of buildings erected by the kings, and of expeditions undertaken at their command, are not unfrequent ; several of the latter the reader will meet with later on. The most important report of all is that which Ramses III (about 1180 to 1148 B. C.) gave of his reign, and which is preserved in the so-called *Papyrus Harris I ;* it is a comprehensive account of Ramses's architectural enterprises, his expeditions, and his gifts to the temples ; in addition it gives a brief review of the state of Egypt immediately before the reign of the king's father, Setnecht. Lists of conquered nations are also of frequent occurrence, but often possess very little value. The most valuable of these lists is that of Thutmosis III, which gives the names of from three hundred to four hundred conquered nations and cities, lying mostly in Asia. Later lists, as those of Seti I and Ramses II, enumerating over a hundred countries, and that of Sheshong I, which gives an equal number, are frequently copied in part from the lists of Thutmosis III, and can be used only with the utmost caution. The oldest example of such a list is a stele of Usertesen I, which enumerates the negro tribes conquered by him. Scarabæi are seldom of historical value, though some belonging to the reign of Amenhetep III are important, viz., those noticing his marriage with Queen Tii, and those giving accounts of his hunting exploits. Of great importance are the tombs of the nobles. These tombs had attached to them funereal chapels, the walls of which were covered with paintings and inscriptions, giving a brief biographical sketch of the individual buried in the tomb, enumerating his titles, his possessions, and all his exploits. These inscriptions are of great value. To them we owe all that we know of the Egyptian civilization, and often all the historical knowledge we possess of entire epochs (confer the case of the Una inscription, page 42).

b. Asiatic Sources.—First among these we must mention the *Bible*. The Sacred Writings are, as may be expected from their character, not the most copious or important sources of Egyptian history. The first two books, Genesis and Exodus, frequently mention Egypt, but they are concerned only with the fate of the Hebrews who dwelt in Egypt, and do not go into Egyptian history. In the books of the Kings and in Chronicles frequent allusions are made to Egyptian history, and what we find here is always confirmed by the monuments. The prophets, especially Ezekiel and Jeremias, frequently allude to contemporaneous Egyptian history. Of greater importance are the Assyrian inscriptions. These inscriptions shed light on a period of Egyptian history of which we know nothing from the national monuments. I refer to the period of the Assyrian invasions in the seventh century B. C. The Assyrian kings whose inscriptions are of importance in this connection are Tiglathpilesar III, Sargon II, Sanherib, and Assurbanipal. Next in importance are the inscriptions of King Nebuchadnezzar II, of Babylon, who invaded Egypt in the sixth century B. C.

c. Classical Sources.—Of the host of classical writers who wrote on Egypt I give in the following only the principal ones. The book that long stood unchallenged as a source of Egyptian history is the "*Historiæ*" of *Herodotus of Halicarnassus*. The study of the monuments has, however, revealed great errors in this work, and has proved it to be utterly untrustworthy as a history. Herodotus's great fault was that he believed all the stories his guides told him, some of which are so improbable that we are surprised to find that so intelligent a man as our author was should have believed them at all. He visited Egypt about 450 B. C., at a time when it was under Persian rule, and probably never got farther south than Memphis. What he saw he described accurately, and that part of his history which relates to the times of the last Psametichs and the Persian rulers of the land is perfectly reliable. His book is the book of a tourist, and all his faults are the faults of a tourist who travels in a

strange and wonderful land without any knowledge of the
language, and having but a short time to "do "the sights.
Another reason why the book is in great part unreliable
is because the Greeks, believing the Egyptians possessed
of a deep and mysterious learning, and having some dim
tradition of the fact that their arts and sciences were originally derived from Egypt, though they had already far
surpassed their teachers, sought to derive their entire
civilization—their religion and philosophy, which were
purely native, as well as art and science, which had indeed received their first impulse from Egypt—from the
mystic lore of that most ancient land. The Egyptian
priests with whom the Greek tourists came into contact
naturally strengthened them in this belief, and gave themselves a very mysterious air, thus still more increasing
their reputations for learning. One word on the subject
of castes may well be said here before we leave Herodotus. From his work an erroneous impression has crept
into many modern books on Egypt, that the ancient
Egyptians were divided into so-called "*castes.*" In ancient Egypt there existed, of course, the same classes that
existed in all ancient monarchies. There was the king
and the royal family, the hereditary nobility, the middle
class, consisting of merchants, farmers, mechanics—from
which government officials and priests were recruited as
well as from the princes and nobles—the laborers, and
the slaves. No one was, however, compelled to follow in
the footsteps of his father. Thus, if the father was a government official, a priest, an officer, a merchant, a farmer,
or a mechanic, the son need not necessarily also be a government official, a priest, an officer, a merchant, a farmer,
or a mechanic, but was free to choose his vocation. We
have even instances of men of humble birth rising to the
highest position in the gift of the crown; and that does
not look as though the Egyptians had possessed a system
of castes.

The most important of these writers is *Manetho of
Sebennythos.* He lived in the third century before the
common era, and his book was written about 271 B.C., as
tradition asserts at the instance of Ptolemy Philadelphus.
Manetho was a high priest and temple scribe of Sebennythos, and was thus familiar with the Egyptian language.
He was also an able classical scholar. Thus he was fitted

for the work of writing an Egyptian history as perhaps no other man then living, his learning giving him access alike to the native monuments and the classic authors, the errors of which latter he attacked. The chief value of the work lay in the fact that, being based on the native sources, it must have been quite reliable. Manetho divided all the kings from Mena to Alexander the Great into thirty-one so-called *dynasties*, stating from what part of Egypt the various dynasties came. On what his division is based we can not say. It is important to note that the *Turin Papyrus* makes a somewhat different division from his. He also divided Egyptian history into three periods: I. *Old Empire* (Dynasties I to XI); II. *Middle Empire* (Dynasties XII to XIX); III. *New Empire* (Dynasties XX to XXX). We retain his terms, but make a somewhat different division, as will be seen in the course of this book. Unfortunately, this important work is lost, and only fragmentary extracts of it have been preserved. The historians who made these extracts were not guided by a true scientific spirit, but took only what happened to suit their immediate purpose, and the extracts frequently conflict with one another in important details. These copyists were *Josephus*, the Jewish historian, *Africanus* and *Eusebius*. Of course, we can form no just estimate of a work preserved in so fragmentary a condition. *Diodorus Siculus*, who visited Egypt about 57 B. C., wrote an account of the country. His work is, however, but little more trustworthy than that of Herodotus. Diodorus seems to have had all of Herodotus's faults but none of his virtues. Manetho he does not seem to have known; at all events he does not refer to his book. *Strabo* and *Pliny* both touch Egyptian history incidentally, but are not trustworthy. *Plutarch*, who lived in the second century A. D., wrote a fair work on Egyptian religion, under the title of " *Peri Isidos kai Osiridos.*" *Horapollon Nilous* wrote between the years 379 and 395 A. D., a work under the title "*Hieroglyphica,*" in which he gives mostly correct explanations of such hieroglyphics as frequently occur in Ptolemaic inscriptions. He knew, however, merely the ideographic and not the phonetic value of these hieroglyphs.

§ 3. *Prehistoric Conditions.*

When we first come upon Egypt, it is a full-grown state possessed of a well-ordered government, a well-organized society, and a civilization of a high order. At the dawn of history the formative period of the nation was over, and Egypt was a finished product. How many centuries the formative period lasted we can not say, but we can, from facts observed in the later development of the land and its religion, make some deductions as to the prehistoric conditions of the country. We can even—and that is of great importance—trace in general outline the formative process, the result of which was the Egyptian state. Egypt was not always a single united country as it was in historic times, but was for a long time previous to Mena divided into two countries, which were entirely independent of one another, and remained so until King Mena united them and founded the Egyptian state about 3200 B. C. These two countries were known even after the union as "*the North*" and "*the South*," and the official name of the united kingdom was *Taui*—"Both lands"—thus preserving the memory that there were originally two countries where in historical times there was but one. One of the king's titles was *Sam-taui*, uniter of both lands. We can even say what cities were the capitals of the two states. The capital of the South was in all probability the city of *Nechebet*, that of the North was the city of *Buto*. We deduce these facts from the fact that the goddess of *Nechebet*, whose name was also *Nechebet*, was regarded in all epochs of Egyptian history as the tutelar divinity of Upper Egypt (the South), and the goddess of *Buto* (known originally as the double city of *Pe* and *Dep*, and in later times as *Per Ouatj*) *Ouatj* was regarded in all epochs of Egyptian history as the tutelar deity of Lower Egypt (the North). Each of these two countries had its own crown—Lower Egypt a curiously shaped *red* crown, and Upper Egypt a peculiar *white* crown, shaped like one of the pieces used in playing nine-pins. When the two countries were united these two crowns were combined into one as the *peshent*, or double crown—the white crown being put inside of the red.

These two countries were in themselves composite products, resulting from the union of various small districts which we designate as *nomes*. That these nomes were originally independent of one another we can deduce with some degree of.certainty from the fact that they retained their autonomy throngh all epochs of Egyptian history, had their own hereditary rulers, known as *nomarchoi*, their own local governments, and, what is most important in this inquiry, their own peculiar religious beliefs.

Egyptian tradition naturally ignores this state of things, asserting that the first pharaohs of the land were the gods; that on these succeeded the *Shemsu-Hor*, "Followers of Horus '—a sort of demi-gods ; and on these, finally, King Mena. That in Mena's time the two countries were united into one was a fact that could not be spirited away by any amount of tradition ; so a legend arose to explain the fact that the country was divided before Mena's time, that *Horus* and *Set* had divided the country between them. Such a legend which seeks to explain existing conditions we call *aiteological*.

The question whether or not the Egyptians were aborigines has been frequently discussed. The most probable solution of the problem is this: The Egyptians as a race were aborigines, and they always looked upon themselves as such. They designate only their own people as *rometu*, "men"; the other peoples may be Syrians, Negroes, or Asiatics, but "*men*" they are not. It seems probable, however, that these aborigines were subdued by a small band of invaders who came from southwestern Asia, and who, though not strong enough to influence the race, yet were sufficiently powerful to force on the conquered people their language, and perhaps some of their religious conceptions. The relations between conqueror and conquered were then pretty much the same as those between the Anglo-Saxons and aboriginal Britons, and those between the conquering Arabs and the modern Egyptians. Of course, this is merely a hypothesis, though it is a very probable one. ·

To speak of a " Stone age " in prehistoric Egypt is entirely out of the way. Stone implements were used for many centuries even in historic times, and the " Stone age "—if we may speak of one at all—falls within the historic periods.

§ 4. *A Brief Sketch of the Ancient Egyptian Religion.*

To understand the development of Egyptian religion we must understand the prehistoric conditions sketched above, and must have a thorough knowledge of Egyptian history. We would, therefore, advise our readers to read the history before they read this sketch of the religion of Egypt.

The Egyptians were originally what is called *animists;* that is to say, they believed that, just as man is endowed with a soul, so every animal, every plant, ay, every inanimate object is also endowed with a soul, or rather is possessed of a spirit or demon which is the cause of the good or evil qualities the animal, plant, or thing in question possesses. The animal, plant, or thing in question thus hecame the object of a primitive cult with a view to propitiating the same. The two great motives of primitive cults are always *love* and *fear*, and of the two fear is the stronger. The savage is quicker at propitiating an evil spirit in order to preserve himself from harm than at showing gratitude to a benignant one. The early Egyptians worshiped animals and trees with especial fervor. Of the tree cult we do not know more than that every nome had its sacred trees; that the sycamore was sacred to the goddess Hathor, and that one of the gods bore the name *Cheri-baqef*, " He-in-his-oil-tree "—i. e., the spirit dwelling in the oil-tree. Of the animal worship we know a little more. Both motives of primitive cults, love and fear, must have operated on the Egyptian mind in this cult. The evil spirits that dwell in the lion, the crocodile, the hippopotamus, must be propitiated, and to this end the animal must be worshiped; the primitive mind can not abstract the spirit from the animal it has chosen for a dwelling-place. Again, it can scarce have been fear that impelled the worship of the bull, the cow, and such useful scavengers as the ibis, the vulture, and the sparrow-hawk. Even in later times, when animism no longer prevailed, some traces of this early animal cult still remained in that various animals were looked upon as sacred to the gods. How the sacred animals came to be connected with their divinities we do not undertake to say. We shall here confine ourselves to an enumeration of the various sacred animals. The oldest and chief of these were the Apis-bull, sacred to Ptah, and the Mnevis-bull, sacred to Rāharmachis; the cow was sacred to Isis, Hathor, and Nephthys; the ram to Amon and Chnum; the cat to Rā, Sōchet, Bast, and Tefnut; the lion to Pō-chet and Sōchet; the ibis and cynocephalus were sacred to Thot; the jackal was sacred to Anubis, the sparrow-hawk to Horus, the vulture to Nechebet, the asp to Ouatj, and the crocodile to Sebek. Frequently the deities were depicted with the heads of their sacred animals. Thus Horus always has the head of a sparrow-hawk, Chnum that of a ram, Thot that of an ibis; Nephthys and Hathor are cow-headed, a solar disk being fixed between the horns. Other examples could be given, but these will suffice.

From this early animism was developed in the course of time a *polydæmonism*—i. e., a belief in many demons or spirits. This is the second stage in religious develop-ment; the spirit has been abstracted from the animal, plant, or thing it inhabited and possessed, and has been given a separate, independent existence. From this *poly-dæmonism* was later on developed *polytheism*, or the be-lief in many gods. How these changes came about we can not say; for, when we first come upon the Egyptian religion, it has gone through all of these stages, but it has retained numerous traces of this early development. This development must have taken place in the various nomes before their union and independently in each, for they pre-sent to us very varied religious beliefs. Each nome had its own peculiar local divinities and its own local theosophy. The head of the local pantheon had his temple in the local capital. These *local* divinities were all supreme in their own localities, and it is *them* that the people worshiped, whatever divinity might be the head of the *national* pan-theon. Every house had attached to it a chapel, in which the local divinities were worshiped. These local deities were all, as a matter of policy, recognized by the national government as the guardian deities of their respective localities. The national religion was, in return, recognized by the various local governments, and the head of the national pantheon had dedicated to him a chapel in each of the local temples. The various religions of these nomes, all in themselves polytheistic, united after the union to form that composite whole—the Egyptian religion—

which we may well designate as an *agglomerated poly-theism.* Thus we see that, just as from the union of the nomes, and, finally, of Upper and Lower Egypt, resulted the Egyptian state, so from a union of the local relig-ions of these nomes resulted the Egyptian religion. It has been already mentioned above that *Nechebet* was re-garded as the guardian divinity of the South and *Ouatj* as that of the North.

In many localities the head of the local pantheon had associated with him two other divinities, who shared his eminence and formed with him what we call a *triad.* Such a triad consisted generally of father, mother, and son. Thus, the triad of Memphis embraced *Ptah,* his wife *Sôchet,* and their son *Imhôtep ;* that of Abydos, *Osiris,* his wife *Isis,* and their son *Horus ;* and that of Thebes, *Amon,* his wife *Mut,* and their son *Chonsu.* But we also find triads consisting of one male and two female mem-bers—possibly father, mother, and daughter—e. g., that of Elephantine : *Chnum, Satet,* and *Anuket.*

Another combination of gods is the *ennead,* or circle of nine gods. The ennead first appears in the fourth Dynasty (about 3000 B. C.). It consists of nine members, com-bined in an apparently arbitrary manner : 1. *Shu ;* 2. *Tefnut ;* 3. *Qeb ;* 4. *Nut ;* 5. *Osiris ;* 6. *Isis ;* 7. *Horus ;* 8. *Set ;* 9. *Nephthys ;* where *Shu* and *Tefnut* are broth-er and sister, *Qeb* and *Nut* man and wife, parents of *Osiris, Isis, Set,* and *Nephthys ; Osiris, Iris,* and *Horus* are father, mother, and son ; and *Set* and *Nephthys* man and wife. The ennead was originated by the priests of On-Heliopolis in order to bring into closer connection the various local religions. These priests claim that it was originated by *Tum,* a solar deity, who was in Heliopolis considered the *leader* of the ennead, though standing out-side of it. In fact, the ennead, which had national ac-ceptance, was everywhere assigned a different deity, the head of the local pantheon as leader, though its member-ship remained fixed, except that in later times *Set* was eliminated, and *Horwer,* a form of the god Horus, or *Thot,* put in his place.

To many of the Egyptian gods there has been ascribed a *cosmological origin.* Thus *Ptah* of Memphis and *Chnum* of Elephantine were in the very first line con-sidered as *world-builders,* or, to use the scientific term, as *lexiurgoi*, while the priests of On-Heliopolis ascribed the same function to *Rā* and *Tum*. But we must not wonder at this multitude of world-builders. It is but consistent with the entire character of the Egyptian religion; it is but natural that the important office of world-builder should be ascribed in every locality to the head of the local pantheon.

These were not, however, the cosmological gods proper. There was a number of other gods of undoubted cosmological origin that had not the slightest connection with any pantheon, some of which were worshiped by the people generally, while others were mere speculative deities, the full import of which was known to the priesthood alone. One of the chief divinities of the former class was *Ranutet*, the goddess of the harvest, who was recognized and worshiped throughout the land. She had her chapels in the granaries and her altars in the open field, and was ardently worshiped by the great land-owners as well as by the small farmers. Of her official cult we know nothing. Another popular cosmological figure was *Hāpi*, the god of the Nile, of whose cult in the times of the New Empire (B. C. 1530-1050) we are well informed. Hundreds of hymns addressed to him have come down to us, all expressing a fervent devotion and sincere gratitude for his many good offices. Thousands of statuettes representing the god have also been preserved. With time he assumed a national importance rivaled only by the heads of the great national religions, *Ptah*, *Rā*, *Osiris*, and *Amon*. This is but natural, for it is to this stream that Egypt owes all its prosperity — ay, its very existence. *Min*, the agricultural god of *Qebti* (Coptos, fifth Upper Egyptian nome), also belongs to this class of divinities. A typical representative of the second class is *Chepra*, the god of the mysterious Becoming; he was a purely theosophical figure, and had no hold on the popular mind.

Results of cosmological speculation are likewise the "eight gods of the elements," so called—the *ogdoas* of *Chmunu-Hermopolis*, the home of *Thot*. They appear in four couples: 1. *Nun* and *Nut*; 2. *Heh* and *Hehet*; 3. *Kek* and *Keket*; and 4. *Nenu* and *Nenut*. Originally there were only the four male divinities, as they appear in the paintings on the walls of the tomb of Seti I (died about

1300 B. C.) ; the goddesses are later additions, their names being merely the feminine forms of those of the male divinities. The meaning ascribed to them is this: 1. *Nun* is the male generative principle of the universe, the father of *Rā*, *Nut* is the female conceptive principle, while together they personify the original chaos; 2. *Heh* and *Hehet* personify eternity ; 3. *Kek* and *Keket*, darkness; and, 4. *Nenu* and *Nenut*, moisture. The full development of this curious cosmological doctrine seems to belong to a later theosophy. Another cosmological couple are *Shu* and his sister *Tefnut*. *Shu* is the god that supports the heavens, and is, in all probability, a personification of the atmosphere. His sister *Tefnut* owes her existence merely to the desire of giving every god a female companion. *Qeb* and *Nut*, his wife, are also a cosmological couple. He is a personification of the earth, she of the heavens. They are given a place in one of the acknowledged national religions as parents of *Osiris*, *Isis*, *Set*, and *Nephthys* (Egyptian name, *Nebhat*).

There were several deities that owed their existence to pure speculation and had, as a rule, no connection with the pantheons. The most important of these was *Māt*, the goddess of truth and justice, who is the personification of these qualities. She had national importance as lady-patroness of justice and its ministers, the judges, who were all priests of *Māt*. There is little reason to doubt the statement of Herodotus that the judges wore her picture on their breasts. Of her cult, however, we know nothing. *Sāfchet*, the goddess of wisdom, of which she is a personification, was regarded as the wife of *Thot*, and was no doubt a very old figure in the theosophy of Chmunu-Hermopolis. *Thot* himself is a result of speculation, the personification of learning and wisdom ; the scribe of the gods, and as such the patron of scribes. He has in this capacity national recognition. His home, Chmunu, seems to have been a great seat of speculative theosophy.

Besides these many divinities—and our space has not permitted us to name more than the most important ones—untold legions of demons, some attached to a particular pantheon, others floating about in wild and unrestrained freedom, help to complicate the religion. Osiris alone had *forty-two* demons attached to his person as associate

judges in the court that sat in the Lower World—in that
part of it known as the "hall of the two truths"—and
tried the departed souls to judge of their worthiness to
enter the blessed abodes. Each of these had a peculiarly
absurd name, which the dead man had to know and to
each one he had to make a special negative confession.
Besides these forty-two judges, unnumbered good and evil
spirits peopled the Lower World, all of which the dead
man had to know and name at sight. It is only of these
spirits of the *Amenti*, as the Egyptians called the Lower
World, that we know the names and, to some extent, the
natures. It was, by the by, far more important to know
the former than the latter, for by merely calling him by
name the dead man could bring to his aid a good spirit or
exorcise an evil one. To *know* the demon was to have
power over him, so that the outlook of the poor soul was
not so bad, after all. The rite of circumcision, so exten-
sively practiced by the ancient Egyptians, has been brought
into connection with this belief in demons. It is conject-
ured that this rite was originally a substitute for human
sacrifice which may have been practiced in prehistoric
times.

Now, we inquire in what relation the various local religions stood to one another. Part of them remained in
obscurity, having only local significance ; part came with
time to have national import ; and it is now our object to
inquire into the cause of this. Eight of these religions
came with time to have national sway : those of *Ptah* of
Memphis, of *Rā* of Heliopolis, *Osiris* of Abydos, *Amon*
of Thebes, *Sebak* of Crocodolilopolis, *Neit* of Sais, *Hathor*
of Denderah, and *Horus* of Edfu. The causes of this lay
partly in the character of the religion itself, partly in the
history of the nation. Three religions seem to have come
into prominence much at the same time : those of *Rā*,
Osiris, and *Ptah*. *Rā* owes his early prominence to the
fact that he was *the* solar deity *par excellence*; he was
looked upon as the first divine king of Egypt. His religion is of peculiar interest to us, for it finally culminated
in a solar monotheism under Amenhetep IV (about 1382–
1370 B. C.), who set up *Aten*, the solar disk, as the supreme and, to a certain extent, the only god of Egypt.
After the suppression of this reform, *Rā* seems rapidly to
have lost his national prestige, and to have sunk to the

rank of the local deity of Heliopolis, becoming merged with *Amon* as *Amon-Rā*. *Osiris* also owes his early prominence to religious reasons. He was god of the dead, the ruler of the *Amenti*, and as such was a prominent figure in all epochs of Egyptian history. Together with him, *Horus*, and his mother *Isis*, and *Nebhat* (Nephthys), the sister of Osiris, came into prominence. *Set*, his brother, gained an unenviable notoriety through the Osiris mythology, as the evil god—the great enemy of his brother Osiris. *Anubis* is also drawn into the circle by being made the son of *Osiris* and *Nebhat*. *Ptah* was originally merely the head of the Memphitic pantheon, and as such was no more than the head of any other local pantheon. The rise of Mena, however, the union of the North and South, and the fact that through this union Memphis became the capital of the united kingdom, gave him a commanding place in the national pantheon. He became the god of the government, and, as such, the chief god of the nation; and, even after *Amon* had succeeded him in this position, he held a high place in the religion until, under the Ptolemies, he was merged with *Osiris* into the new god *Serapis*, who was imported from Asia Minor and given out as a union of *Osiris* and the *Apis-bull*, the sacred animal of *Ptah*. At the close of the Old Empire (about 2400 B.C.) there is a gap in Egyptian history, and it is not until 2100 B.C. that we again stand on firm ground, and then it is Thebes that is the capital of Egypt; and, as a consequence, the head of its local pantheon, *Amon*, a deity hitherto obscure, is the official head of the national pantheon. He retained this position throughout the eleventh and twelfth dynasties, but in the thirteenth dynasty (about 1930 B.C.) he seems to have surrendered the supremacy to *Sebak*, of Crocodilopolis in the Fayoum. *Sebak* did not retain his position long, for the thirteenth dynasty ended in anarchy, and soon after its fall the *Hyksos* invaded Egypt. For several centuries the foreign invaders ruled supreme; but about 1530 B.C. they were driven out by Aahmes I, a Theban king, and Thebes again became the capital of Egypt. As one consequence of this, Amon again became the official head of the pantheon. But about 1400 B.C. he was again dethroned, when King Amenhetep IV (Chuenaten) instituted the religious reform above mentioned. Unfortunately, the reform was short-lived, dying soon after its founder. Again, *Amon*, now called *Amon-Rā*, ruled supreme. Through all the vicissitudes of Egyptian history he held his own, even extending his sway to the neighboring kingdom of Napata, founded in Ethiopia early in the tenth century B. C., probably by the descendants of the priest-kings of Dynasty XXI, who had been driven from Egypt by Sheshong I, until, finally, when Psemtek I founded the twenty-sixth dynasty, he gave way to *Neit* of Sais. She seems to have retained the place at the head of the national pantheon until the times of the Ptolemies, when *Hathor* of Denderah and *Horus* of Edfu shared the supremacy with *Serapis*. They, too, finally passed away with the advent of Christianity. Alone of all the old deities *Isis* retained her sway, even in Christian times, well into the fourth century A. D. on the Island of Philæ; but she, too, finally yielded, and passed away before the new religion.

Such is as adequate a sketch of the Egyptian religion as can be given in the space allotted. The reader will observe that the religion was not a homogeneous whole, the result of a continuous development along one line of thought, but a heterogeneous mass, the resultant of the union of a large number of religions, each of itself *polytheistic* in nature; and that with so little fusion of the component parts that we have all through the history of this curious religion *three* or *four*—and in later times as many as *eight*—essentially different religions having *national recognition* and a large number of *local religions* running side by side. The reader will further observe that there is *no trace* of an "*original monotheism*," and that the monotheism which was developed from the *Rā*-religion was a very imperfect one, and was, far from being "original," the result of many centuries of thought and speculation.

CHAPTER II.

§ 1. *The First Dynasty.*

Mena (3200 B. C.).—The great king who first united
Upper and Lower Egypt into one country lived not *later*
than 3200 B. C. How many years *earlier* he lived we have
no means of saying; he may have lived five hundred or
even a thousand years earlier; but, until we can assign
him an accurately correct date, it is best to retain the one
here given. Naturally he occupies a high place in Egyptian tradition, being regarded as the first human king of
the country. His birthplace was the small town of *Teni*
(Greek, *This*), near Abydos. This town was not, however, favorably located for the capital of a great empire;
so Mena left it, and removed the seat of the government
to the city of Memphis, which lay on the Nile a little to
the south of the apex of the Delta. This city was the
home of the god *Ptah*, who thus became the official head
of the Egyptian pantheon. The site of this city was on
the left bank of the Nile, a little above the modern city of
Cairo. At the modern village of Mitrahine a few mounds
of rubbish and some scattered ruins still mark the place
where once stood one of the greatest and richest cities of
all antiquity. The Egyptian name of the city was *Men-
nefer*—"the good (or beautiful) abode "—from which the
Greek name Memphis, by which we designate the city,
was derived. Every city of ancient Egypt had two names
—a *common or profane name* and a *sacred name*, derived
either from the name of its god or from some mythological
event located at it. The sacred name of *Men-nefer* was
Het-ka-Ptah, "the abode of the spirit of *Ptah.*" It was

defended by a citadel called " *anbuhetj*," " the white wall."
The city itself was probably far older than the time of
Mena; but, in transferring the capital to it, the king naturally greatly enlarged it, and came to be considered,
first, its benefactor, and later on its founder. What we
know of this king has come to us through the Greek historians and Manetho. All that is usually ascribed to the
founders of empire is ascribed to him. The legends related of him are mostly absurd. He is said to have
founded the temple of *Ptah* at Memphis, which was the
first Egyptian temple, to have first organized the temple
ritual, and to have introduced the cult of the *Apis-bull*—
all of which stories are alike incredible. As above noted,
Memphis and its cult existed long before Mena's time.
He is also said to have invented the alphabet. The most
absurd story is that told by Diodorus, who relates that the
king had once upon a time, when pursued by his own
hounds, fled into Lake Mœris, and had been brought to
shore by a crocodile; and, in gratitude for this rescue, he
had built Crocodilopolis on the lake-shore, had instituted
the crocodile-cult, and given over the lake to these sauri-
ans. Then he had built a pyramid here for his tomb, and
had founded the celebrated labyrinth. In reality the
" lake " did not yet exist in these early times, having been
built by Amenhetep III almost two thousand years
later. Crocodilopolis, the pyramid, and the labyrinth were
built by this same pharaoh.* Almost as absurd is the
legend that he was an effeminate king, devoted to the
pleasures of the table, and had first taught his subjects
to take a reclining posture while eating. In the first place,
founders of empire are not made of such stuff; and, in the
second place, the custom in Egypt was not to *recline*, but
to *sit* at table. The king is also represented as a patron
of poets. More trustworthy is what Manetho tells us of
this king. He was a mighty warrior, who campaigned in
Lybia, and was killed by a hippopotamus. This agrees
well with what we would expect of a founder of empire
—he was a warlike ruler, and was killed while hunting.
According to Manetho, he ruled about sixty years.

---

* The word pharaoh, which was taken over into the modern
languages from the Bible, is derived from the Egyptian word *perāa*
—" the great house "—a common designation of the king.

Teta, whom the Greek writers called *Atothis I*, succeeded Mena. According to the extract from Manetho,
made by Africanus, he ruled fifty-seven years ; according
to that made by Eusebius, he reigned only twenty-seven.
Manetho relates that he built the citadel of Memphis, and
wrote a work on anatomy. This latter notice is to some
extent confirmed by a passage of the medical " Papyrus
Ebers," in which a hair-restorer is said to have been invented by *Shesh*, the mother of our ruler. A two-headed
crane is said to have appeared in his reign—a phenome-
non that presaged a long period of prosperity. Of Atet
(*Atothis II*), whom Manetho called *Kenkenes*, nothing is
known beyond the fact that he ruled thirty-two years. In
the reign of Ata, the *Ouenephes* of Manetho, who ruled
twenty-three years, a great famine prevailed in Egypt. He
is said to have erected a pyramid at Kochome, near Saqqarah. Hesepti, the *Usaphaïdes* of Manetho, who ruled
twenty years, is quite a literary character among these
kings. A remedy for leprosy, which was afterward copied
in a medical papyrus preserved in Berlin and in the " Papyrus Ebers," is said to date from his reign. Numerous
copies of the sixty-fourth chapter of the " Book of the
Dead " assert that this chapter was " discovered " in his
reign, and not in that of Mycerinos, while all copies agree
that the one hundred and thirtieth chapter dates from this
reign. Merbapen, the *Miebidos* of Manetho, reigned
nineteen years. He must have been quite an important
ruler, for the list of kings discovered at Saqqarah begins
with his name. Semenptah, the *Semempses* of Manetho, ruled eighteen years. It is related that many mira-
cles took place in his reign, and that a great plague almost
depopulated the land. Of Kebhu, the *Bienches* of
Manetho, we know only that he ruled twenty-six years.

§ 2. *The Second Dynasty.*

Neterbau, the *Betjau* of the list of kings found at
Abydos, the *Boethos* of Manetho, reigned thirty-eight
years. Manetho relates that during his reign an earth-
quake at Bubastis swallowed up many people. Kakau,
the *Kaichos* of Manetho, reigned twenty-nine years. According to Manetho, he introduced the cult of the *Apis-bull*
at Memphis, that of the *Menevis-bull* at Heliopolis, and

that of the *ram* at Mendes.   This legend is incredible
and unhistorical.   These cults were all as old as the cities
in which they were practiced, and antedated the union of
the two countries by many centuries,   Ba-en-neter,
whom Manetho calls *Binothris*, reigned forty-seven years.
He seems to have been an important lawgiver. If we can
credit the account of Manetho, it was this pharaoh who
first legalized the succession in the female line.   This was
of great importance throughout the course of Egyptian
history, for according to this law a woman could sit on
the Egyptian throne, and many a dynasty based its right
to the throne on the law of female succession. Of Ouat-
jnes, the *Tlas* of Manetho, we know only that he reigned
seventeen years.   Sent, called *Sethenes* by Manetho, who
ruled forty-one years, is said to have revised a medical
treatise written in the reign of *Hesepti*. Perabsen,
possibly the *Chaires* of Manetho, reigned seventeen years.
Neferkara, the *Nephercheres* of Manetho, is said to
have ruled twenty-five years.   Under him, Manetho says,
the Nile ran honey for eleven days.—Maspero, following
Mariette, places in this dynasty some monuments, which
are certainly older than the times of the fourth dynasty.
They are few in number, but show certain striking peculiarities which prove that they belong together.   But we can
not fully verify this very plausible hypothesis until we have
more of these monuments.   For the present it is certainly
better not to ascribe them to any particular period, but to
say merely that they are older than the times of the fourth
dynasty.   The same may be said of the great Sphinx of
Gizeh, the age of which is unknown.

§ 3. *The Third Dynasty.*

How the second dynasty came to an end and the third
ascended the throne we do not know ; in fact, our knowledge of the first three dynasties is limited to the names of
the rulers and a few legends.   Neferkasokar was the
first king of this dynasty.   Manetho calls him *Nechero-
phes*, and ascribes to him a reign of twenty-eight years.
The same historian relates that in this reign the Lybians
revolted ; but, as the battle was about to begin, they
became frightened at seeing the moon apparently greatly
enlarged, and fled from the field.   Tosorthos ruled

twenty-nine years. Manetho relates that he was a great builder, and had perfected the system of writing. He was also a great physician, and for this reason had been identified with Asclepios by the Greeks. Of the other rulers of this dynasty we know only the names. Huni, the last of these kings, the *Kerpheres* of Manetho, who ruled twenty-six years, was the immediate predecessor of King *Snefru*, the founder of the fourth dynasty.

§ 4. *The Fourth Dynasty—The Pyramid-Builders, about 2830–2700* B. C.

Snefru (2830–2806 B. C.), the founder of the fourth dynasty, ascended the throne about 2830 B. C. The change of dynasty seems to have been peaceably accomplished. "Papyrus Prisse," the only text that refers to it, remarks: "Then King Huni died, and King Snefru became a beneficent ruler over the entire land." He is the first king from whose reign monuments have come down to us. He and his successors built for their tombs great pyramids, forming a line miles in length, from Gizeh on the north to Meydoum on the south. King Snefru, in all probability, is buried in the pyramid of Meydoum, about which lie the tombs of many of his courtiers. The Egyptian name of the pyramid was *Chā*; its builder was *Henka*. Of historical events of this reign we know but little. A legendary papyrus preserved in St. Petersburg tells of an incursion of the Asiatic Bedouins known as *Amu*. To guard against these inroads a line of forts was established stretching across the Egyptian part of the Isthmus of Suez. This string of forts is frequently mentioned in the texts and its official name *anbu hequ*, "Wall of the princes," gave rise to the mistaken impression that the Egyptians had built a wall across their eastern frontier. One of these forts, named after King Snefru, *Aa Snefru*, is mentioned in the memoirs of a noble who lived over a thousand years later. But King Snefru was not content with repelling the inroads of the Asiatics. He was bent on enlarging his empire. On the Sinai peninsula there were located rich copper and malachite mines which the Egyptions worked in very early times. Whether Snefru was the first king who opened these mines, or whether they had been opened to the Egyptians by some previous king,

4

we do not undertake to say, but it is a fact that he is the first king of whom monuments have been found on the peninsula. Inscriptions at both of the great mining camps at Sarbût el Châdem and Wâdi Maghara tell of the king's campaigns against the Bedouins of the region, who were called *Mentiu Satet*, and who seem to have seriously resented the encroachment of the Egyptians. They were of course beaten, but could never be wholly subdued, and gave much trouble in later reigns. Snefru died after a prosperous reign of twenty-four years.

Chufu (2806-2782 B. C.).—When Snefru died he left to his oldest son and successor a great and flourishing kingdom. This king is the *Cheops* of Herodotus. He is the builder of the largest of the three great pyramids of Gizeh, the measurements of which are : side of square base, originally 764 feet, at present 746 feet ; perpendicular height, originally 480 feet, now 450 feet ; and height of slope, originally 611 feet, at present 568 feet. Inside of this great mass of solid masonry there is the chamber in which the sarcophagus of the king was deposited. This chamber is approached by a series of narrow passages, which were, after the sarcophagus was in place, blocked up in a very ingenious manner. The Egyptian name of this pyramid was *Chut*. I may here mention some general facts which hold good for all the pyramids of Gizeh. Each one had connected with it a funereal temple dedicated to the memory of the king buried in the pyramid. All of the pyramids were built *as planned*, a fact that the recent measurements of W. Flinders Petrie have demonstrated beyond a doubt. Thus the old theory that every king when he ascended the throne began a pyramid of moderate proportions, and gradually enlarged it as he found he had the time, is exploded. The reader will find a full *exposé* of these facts in Mr. Petrie's admirable book, "The Pyramids and Temples of Gizeh." About each pyramid lay a number of smaller pyramids, probably the tombs of the members of the royal families, as well as the tombs of the nobles that had lived at the court.

This king was a great builder, the temple of the " Lady of the Pyramids, Isis," and the foundation of the temple of Hathor at Denderah are attributed to him. Two cities —*Menāt-Chufu* (the modern Minye, north of Hermopolis) and *Chufukebet*—bear his name. Like his predecessor, he was compelled to make a campaign against the *Mentiu Satet,* on the Sinai peninsula, who it seems had again begun to molest the Egyptian miners.

The classical accounts of this king are all unreliable. Herodotus gives him a reign of fifty years, and Manetho says he reigned sixty-three, while we know from the Turin Papyrus that he ruled only twenty-four years. The classical historians would also have him appear as a great tyrant, who closed the temples in order that the Egyptians might all labor continuously at his pyramid, and who, when money failed him, prostituted his own daughter in order to raise funds. The chief responsibility for these stories rests on Herodotus. Manetho attempts to reconcile history and legend by relating that the king, whom he calls *Souphis,* had repented in his old age, and had written a book that was regarded as sacred.

Radedef (2782-2759 B. C.).—The son and successor of Chufu, who ruled twenty-three years, did not build a pyramid. Why he departed from the custom begun by his two predecessors we can not say; perhaps the forces and resources of the kingdom were otherwise employed. We know, however, absolutely nothing of this comparatively long reign.

Chafra (2758-2750 B. C.), the *Chephren* of Herodotus, is the builder of the second great pyramid of Gizeh, the Egyptian name of which is *Ouer,* "the Great One." This pyramid is somewhat smaller than that of Chafra's father, Chufu, but it is still of respectable size. Its dimensions are: Length of side of square base originally, 707 feet, now 690 feet; perpendicular height originally, 454¼ feet, now 447 feet; inclined height originally, 572 feet, at present 563 feet. Like all the other pyramids of Gizeh, this one is built of blocks of limestone taken from the quarries of *Turah* (Egyptian name, *Roău*), in the hills on the east bank of the Nile, opposite Memphis. All the pyramids were built so that their sides resembled great steps, and then these steps were filled in with granite blocks, so placed that they formed a smooth, continuous inclined surface. Part of this coating of granite is still left on the upper part of this pyramid. Before this pyramid, a little to the south of the great Sphinx, there stands a large temple built of granite and alabaster, which was most probably erected at Chafra's order. The fact that it stands in front of his pyra-

mid proves conclusively that it was built after that structure. In a well in the interior of this temple were found
the fragments of nine exquisitely wrought diorite statues
of the king. Seven of these are at present in the museum
of Boulaq, one of them being almost unharmed. How
these statues got in the well we do not know. The temple itself is also a mystery; it may have been Chafra's
funereal temple, but it may just as well have been erected
to the Sphinx, the image of *Rāharmachis*, or to any
other deity. Of him also the classical historians relate
that he was a great tyrant, who systematically oppressed
his subjects in order to be able to complete his great pyramid; but there is absolutely no foundation for these
stories. He died after a reign of only eight years.

Menkaurā (2749-2724 B. C.), the *Mycerinos* of
Herodotus, succeeded Chafra. Herodotus tells us this
pharaoh was celebrated for his great piety and righteous-
ness, and the Egyptian monuments bear this out. They
tell us that he sent out his son *Hordedef* to inspect the
temples of the land, and that while on this tour of inspection the prince had "discovered" the sixty-fourth chapter
of the "Book of the Dead" at Hermopolis (*Chmunu*).
Some copies of the thirtieth chapter of the same compila-
tion state that it also was "found" in this reign. Several
later texts mention this prince; the celebrated "Minstrel's
Song" quotes one of his sayings, and a letter written in
the time of Ramses II speaks of the difficulty of understanding his writings. The story, related by some Greek
authors, that the oracle of Buto had predicted to him that
he would die young, and that he had consequently spent
day and night in dissipation in order to double his life, is
utterly untrustworthy. His tomb is the third and smallest
of the pyramids of Gizeh. Its dimensions are: Side of
square base, 354½ feet; perpendicular height, originally
218 feet, now 203 feet; height of incline, originally 278
feet, now 261 feet. The order to erect this structure and
the account of the work are given in an unfortunately extremely mutilated inscription in one of the tombs of Gizeh.
The name of the pyramid was *Heri*. Although a sys-
tematic attempt to destroy this pyramid was made in 1196
A. D., it is the best preserved of all the pyramids of Gizeh.
In the chamber Vyse found the stone sarcophagus and
fragments of the wooden mummy-case of this king. The

former was lost in a shipwreck; the latter are preserved in the British Museum. How long this pharaoh ruled we can not say, as the Turin Papyrus has a break at his name. We must, therefore, for the present take the years given by the most trustworthy of the classical writers, Manetho, who states the king ruled twenty-five years.

Shepseskaf (2723–2701 B. C.).—Of this king we know very little. An interesting description was found in the tomb of his favorite, *Ptahshepses.* This man was born in the reign of Menkaurā, and was educated together with the royal princes. His career as an official falls almost entirely within *Shepseskaf's* reign. This king gave his favorite his daughter *Māatchā* in marriage, and heaped honors upon him. It is a characteristic fact that neither in this biography nor in any other inscription of this time do we meet with any mention of warlike expeditions. The monuments, however, make frequent mention of the king's trips through the country, of festivals, and of buildings erected by the pharaoh. Herodotus tells us that the successor of Mycerinos, whom he calls *Asychis,* built a pyramid of brick, and enlarged the southern peristyle of the Ptah-temple of Memphis. Diodorus, who calls him *Sasychis,* mentions him as one of the five great lawgivers of Egypt. One of his alleged laws is mentioned by Herodotus: allowing a debtor to pawn his father's mummy; in case the mummy were not redeemed, he would lose for himself and family the right of burial. Diodorus also states that this Pharaoh regulated the ritual, and invented geometry and the art of observing the stars. Of these stories it is safe to accept only what relates to the building operations of the king. According to Manetho, he ruled twenty-two years.

Two kings, *Sebercheres* and *Tamphthis,* are mentioned by Manetho as belonging to this dynasty, but their names have not yet been found on the monuments.

§ 5. The Fifth Dynasty (2700–2560 B. C.).

The change of dynasty seems to have been peaceably accomplished, for we find that men who had held office under the preceding dynasty were retained by the kings of the new house. Possibly the direct male line had died out, and the new line came to the throne by the right of female succession.

Userkaf (2700–2693 B. C.), the first king of this dynasty, was the immediate successor of *Shepseskaf*, as is proved by the inscription of *Sechemkarā*, who held official positions under Kings Chafra, Menkaurā, Shepseskaf, Userkaf, and Sahura. All we know of this pharaoh is that he ruled seven years, and was buried in a pyramid called *Abasu*.

Sahurā (2692–2680 B. C.) had to repel inroads of the *Mentiu Satet*, who had again begun to molest the Egyptian miners on the Sinai peninsula. He founded the city of *Persahurā*, north of Esneh, and built a temple to the goddess *Sōchet*, the wife of *Ptah*, in Memphis. His pyramid, *Chāba*, lies north of Abusir. Sahurā ruled twelve years.

Neferarkarā (2679–2672 B. C.), the successor of Sahurā, is called *Kaka* in the list of Abydos. He died after a reign of seven years, and was buried in a pyramid called *Ba*. Of Shepseskarā (2761–2759 B. C.), we know only that he reigned twelve years. Of Ahtes we know nothing. Neferbarā reigned probably ten years. Akauhor is another ruler of whom we know absolutely nothing.

An, whose *prænomon* was *Userenrā*, was the first king to adopt a throne-name. Hitherto the kings had kept the names they had borne as princes, but now the kings took a new name on ascending the throne. This name was always compounded with the name of the god *Rā*, and was the *official name* of the ruler, by which he was designated in all state documents. The name of *Rā* was chosen, in all probability, because this god was considered as the first divine king of Egypt. The king, however, retained his old name, placing before it the title *Sa Rā*, "Son of *Rā*." Thus *An's* name now was King of Upper and Lower Egypt, *User-en-Rā*, the son of *Rā*, *An*. Not content with these two names, the pharaohs took three other names on ascending the throne, answering to the three titles : *Horus, Lord of Both Lands*, and *Horus Nubti*—i. e., "Horus, the conqueror of Set." In olden times the kings used one and the same name with these three titles. Thus, the full name of Amenemhat I was: *The Horus, Nem Mesut* (Renewer of Births), *Lord of Both Lands, Nem Mesut, Horus Nubti, Nem Mesut, King of Upper and Lower Egyyt, Sehōtep-ab-Rā*, the son of Rā, *Amenemhāt.* In later times the Pharaohs took a separate name with each title. Thus, the full name of Ramses II was : *Horus, The strong steer, beloved of Māt, Lord of Both Lands: He that protecteth Egypt and subdueth the Barbarians. Horus Nubti, Rich in years, great in victories, King of Upper and Lower Egypt, Rā user māt setep en Rā* (i. e., Rā, strong in truth, chōsen of Rā), *the son of Rā, Ramessu meri Amon* (Ramses, beloved of Amon). Frequently other titles are added, and the titulature becomes a hymn on the king. *An* warred on the Sinai peninsula with the *Mentiu Satet.* He died after a reign of ten years.

Menkauhor ruled eight years. All we know of him is that he, too, worked the copper and malachite mines of the Sinai. Ded-ka-Ra Assa ruled twenty-eight years. In the fourth year of his reign he sent an expedition to Wadi Maghara on the Sinai. He is the first pharaoh whose name we meet with in the quarries of the Wâdi Hammamât, although undoubtedly already King Chafra worked them. Unas was the last king of this dynasty. With his name the Turin Papyrus concludes a division, and sums up the number of years since Mena, in all six hundred and fifty. It thus would seem that his death marked an epoch in Egyptian history, but our information about this period is so meager that we can not say what great event can have taken place at this time. *Unas* had been appointed co-regent by his father *Assa.* He does not seem to have undertaken any warlike expeditions. He was, however, a great builder, erecting a temple to the goddess *Hathor*, near Memphis ; in the Fayoum there was a city called *Unas* after him, and probably founded by him. The diorite he needed for these works he quarried in Hammamât. After a reign of thirty years the king died.

§ 6. *The Sixth Dynasty (about 2560-2400* B. C.).

Teta was the founder of the new dynasty, and seems to have been the immediate successor of *Unas.* It would seem, however, that the new dynasty did not gain the throne without a struggle ; two kings are mentioned who belong about in this time—*Ati* and *Imhôtep*—both of whom quarried stone in the Wâdi Hammamât. They were most probably pretenders to the crown. *Teta* triumphed over all his rivals, and ascended the throne about 2560 B. C. (?) Whatever struggle there was seems to have been short-lived, and is not mentioned in the inscriptions. These inscriptions are chiefly those of nobles, and though they are, despite their brevity, accurate biographies, recounting the possessions and offices of the nobles they treat of, they touch on matters of state only incidentally. Of the history of this king we know absolutely nothing. Manetho has preserved a legend that he was murdered by one of his body-guard. According to the same historian, he ruled thirty years. This pharaoh was buried in a pyramid near Saqqarah, which was opened in 1881. The Egyptian name of the structure was *Dedasu*. The opening of this pyramid was of the greatest importance for religious history, but of none whatever for secular history, the walls being covered with long religious texts, containing not the slightest historical allusion. After *Teta*, the list of Abydos mentions a King *Ouserkarā*, of whom we know nothing; perhaps this was the king's throne-name, and was put here by mistake.

Merī Rā Pepi (2530–2510 B. C.), who ascended the throne about 2530 B.C., is the greatest monarch of this dynasty. Pepi was the immediate successor of *Teta*, but we do not know whether he was related to his predecessor or not. Pepi's empire embraced all of Egypt and the Sinai peninsula. In the eighteenth year of his reign he sent an expedition to the Wâdi Maghara, and was compelled to punish the *Mentiu*, who had again become troublesome. In the same year he also sent an expedition to *Rôhanu* (Wâdi Hammamât) to quarry stones for some temples he was erecting. His name also appears in the sandstone quarries of Gebel Silsileh, and he is the first king of whose operations here we have any tidings, though assuredly the quarries had been worked by many of his predecessors. We know that he built in Tanis, and an inscription on the walls of the temple of Denderah relates that he had found the old plan of this building prepared in King Chufu's time. He also founded a city, the governor of which, *Bebḁ*, is buried at Shech Said.

The greater part of what we know of his reign is gleaned from the inscription of a noble named *Una*. This noble began his career under King *Teta* in minor offices.

Under Pepi he rapidly gained distinction, rising to high offices. Early in Pepi's reign he was made judge, and acquitted himself so well in a very delicate case that he was given the exalted title of " Only friend to the pharaoh," and was appointed governor of the Nubian district. He now conducted, in conjunction with a justice of lower rank, a case brought by the king against Queen *Amset.* The case was a very delicate one, and conducted with the utmost secrecy ; we do not hear the cause of action, or the outcome of the case. The king was highly pleased with Una's conduct of this case, and heaped new honors upon him. The *Amu Heriusha,* as the Egyptians called the Syrian Bedouins, at this time began to make inroads on Egyptian territory, and it was determined to punish them. A vast army was collected from all parts of Egypt and Nubia, drilled and disciplined under the direction of Una. With this army he marched against the enemy, and in five successive campaigns completely routed them ; their strongholds were taken and destroyed, their crops were burned, their cattle driven off, vast numbers of prisoners were taken, and their country was left completely devastated and almost depopulated. Pepi died soon after the close of this war, after a reign of twenty years, and was buried in his pyramid, which bore the name of *Men-nefer* (the same as that of Memphis). This pyramid, which lies near Saqqarah, was opened in 1881. Its walls are covered with long religious inscriptions.

Mer-en-Rā Horemsāf (2509–2502 B. C.). — On Pepi's death, his son *Merenrā* ascended the throne. Of him we know little outside of what Una tells us. This noble was made a prince by the new ruler, and appointed Governor of the South. In this capacity he highly distinguished himself. He made two enumerations of the South (i. e., twice took the census of his province), a thing that had never been done before, and that gained him great praise from the king. He was then ordered to bring a granite sarcophagus and fittings for the king's pyramid from the quarries at Elephantine. The fact that only one man-of-war was needed to escort six transports and six other vessels is a significant proof of the extent of the Egyptian power in these early times. We have already seen that Pepi I conscripted troops from the Nubian districts bordering on Egypt. In an expedition undertaken

somewhat later Una pressed Nubian tribes into his service
to cut timber and build boats. Most probably these tribes
had been subdued already by King Chufu when he opened
the granite quarries on the First Cataract. These tribes
most probably stood in a relation of semidependence to
Egypt. They certainly retained their tribal relations and
their autonomy, but were compelled to serve in the Egyptian army in case of war, and to assist the expeditions
that were sent to Assuan. Outside of this we know of
this reign only that the king made a tour of inspection on
which he visited the quarries of Assuan, and that he sent
an expedition to the Wâdi Hammamât. According to
Manetho, he ruled only seven years. He was entombed in
his pyramid, which was named *Chānofer*. This pyramid
was opened in 1881, and it was found that the walls were
covered with inscriptions analogous to those found in the
pyramid of his father. In the sarcophagus-chamber was
found the carefully embalmed and well-preserved mummy
of the king, which was brought to Boulaq. The body is
that of a young man, which well accords with the short
reign ascribed to him by Manetho.

Neferkarā, Pepi II (2501–2411 B. C.).—On *Merenrā's* death his brother *Neferkarā* ascended the throne.
He corresponds to Manetho's King *Phiops*, who ruled one
hundred years, as the Turin Papyrus gives *Pepi II* over
ninety years. All that we know of him is that he sent an
expedition to the copper-mines of Wâdi Maghara on the
Sinai. This king was buried in a pyramid near Saqqarah,
the Egyptian name of which was *Men-ānch*. It was
opened in 1881, and contained the same texts as the others. The close of this dynasty is shrouded in darkness.
We know a few of the names belonging here, but of not
one of the kings after Pepi II do we know the history.
Thus we hear of a King *Ment-em-Sāf*, a King *Nefrus*,
and a King *Ab*.

Neitaqer, the *Nitocris* of the classical authors, belongs in this dynasty, though we can not give her her
exact place. Her name is mentioned on none of the monuments, but many a legend is related of her. Herodotus tells
us that, after a reign of scarce one year, King *Menthesou-
phis* was murdered, and his sister and wife, "the beautiful
one with the rosy cheeks," succeeded him. She resolved
to avenge her husband and brother. To this end she had

a great hall built underground which was connected with the waters of the Nile ; the river was prevented from entering by mighty flood-gates. To this hall she invited all who were implicated in the murder of her husband to a banquet. When this was at its height she herself opened the flood-gates, and, the waters of the Nile streaming in, all the guests perished. Then, to avoid the vengeance of the murderers' friends, she threw herself into a large chamber filled with glowing coal and was burned up. The same historian further relates that, in her reign of seven years, she had enlarged the pyramid of Mycerinos, and had coated its apex with granite. There is as little foundation for one of these tales as for the other. The latter story is disproved by the fact that the third pyramid shows no traces of having been rebuilt or enlarged. An Arabic legend is also connected with Nitocris, or, rather, with the third pyramid. To the present day, the Arabs dwelling about the pyramids believe that the ghost of the southern pyramid hovers about it in the shape of a beautiful naked woman. Whom she sets eyes on her smile infatuates ; but she is a great coquette, alternately attracting and repelling her victim until he becomes insane and wanders aimless through the land. Many and many a one, say they, has seen her, especially at noon and sunset, hovering about her pyramid.

CHAPTER III.

§ 1. *The Transition Period—Dynasties VII-XI.*

THIS was a period of frequent revolutions; king after king ascended the throne, but it was a long time before a king arose who succeeded in securing a firm hold on the reins of state. It is next to impossible to give even a chronological list of the kings who ruled in this period, which must have covered some two hundred years, and perhaps more. It is owing to this gap, and one that we shall meet with later, that the chronology of the earlier periods of Egypt is so very uncertain. From conditions existing in the times of the twelfth dynasty it would seem that the great hereditary princes of the realm, the nomarchoi, succeeded in winning some considerable independence during this period. It is but natural that, in a time when the kings felt anything but secure on the throne, they should seek to enlist the support of the nobility, and be ready to purchase that support by according them greater privileges than they had hitherto enjoyed. These nobles were a very shrewd lot, and no doubt made the best of the bargain by selling their support to the highest bidder. It was in all probability this inordinate strengthening of the nobility that finally led to the rise of the Theban princes, and to their accession to the throne under the founder of the eleventh dynasty. This was significant for the entire future of Egypt, as Thebes controlled the destinies of the kingdom for over a thousand years.

Manetho gives only a list of dynasties for this period, as follows :

VII Dynasty: Memphitic, 70 kings in 70 days (according to Eusebius, 5 kings in 75 years).

VIII Dynasty: Memphitic, 27 kings in 146 years.

IX Dynasty: from Heracleopolis, 27 kings in 409 years (Syncellus, 4 kings in 100 years).

X Dynasty: from Heracleopolis, 17 kings in 185 years. Of the names, Manetho gives only that of King *Achthoes*, the founder of the ninth dynasty, of whom he relates that he was the most barbarous and inhuman king that had hitherto ruled in Egypt. He committed many crimes, and was finally stricken with insanity and killed by a crocodile. It is a probable conjecture that Manetho wishes to convey the impression that this king was a foreign invader. In all probability the *Amu Heriusha* whom Una had so effectually crushed had been left alone by *Meri-Rā's* immediate successors, and had again gathered sufficient strength to renew their attacks on Egypt. If this is so, the attack must not have come until after *Neferka-Rā's* long reign. It seems that this time the barbarians had it all their own way, and had finally succeeded in conquering the country. This hypothesis receives some confirmation, however slight, from the fact that a semi-legendary papyrus mentions combats with the *Heriusha* under Kings *Chruti* and *Ameno.* Judging from the names, *Ameno* was probably one of the kings of the eleventh dynasty, and these battles were then fought in delivering Egypt from the foreign invader.

§2. *The Middle Empire, Dynasties XI and XII.*

The Eleventh Dynasty.—With the founder of this dynasty, the Theban princes ascended the throne of Egypt. These kings seem to have delivered Egypt from the yoke of the foreign invader—the war possibly being begun by *Chruti* and *Ameno*—though we nowhere find any mention of this fact. The first of these princes mentioned in the lists of kings is the *erpāti* (i. e., hereditary prince) *Antef.* The three succeeding kings are designated as *Hor*, and the fourth successor of *Antef* is the first one to bear the full titulature of Egyptian kings. From this fact the conclusion has been drawn that the first Antef was merely Prince of Thebes; that his next successors had gradually enlarged their sway until they

ruled over all of Upper Egypt and had assumed the title
Hor—signifying ruler of Upper Egypt; and that, finally,
the fourth successor of Antef had succeeded in conquering all of Egypt, and had consequently assumed the full
titulature of the Egyptian kings. This conjecture is entirely unwarranted. It is probable that these rulers delivered Egypt from the yoke of the foreign invader, but
any attempt to read the history of the war from the titles
of these kings is futile. The founder of the dynasty,
Prince Antef, in all probability was the man with whom
the national movement began, though he possibly died
before other princes had recognized his authority, and
owes his place in the list of kings to the fact that his
dynasty based their claim to the throne on him. To
translate the title of *Hor* as "ruler of Upper Egypt," or
as "duke," is not admissible. *Hor* was one of the titles
of the Egyptian kings. The word signifies *Horus*, and
this title was given the king because he was looked upon
as the "Horus on Earth." The order of succession of
these kings is not certain, and we therefore deem it advisable to group them according to their names. This
will give us two groups, one of kings whose names were
all the same—*Antef*, and another of kings whose names
were all the same—*Mentuhôtep*. Any other arrangement
would be equally arbitrary, while lacking the clearness of
this.

The Antef Kings.—*Antef āa* (i. e., the Great), with
the throne-name *Rā-sechem-up-māt*, is the only king of
this line of whose family relations we have any knowledge.
A note on his sarcophagus informs us that his younger
brother and successor, *Anantef Rā-sechem-herher-māt*,
had the sarcophagus made. This sarcophagus is in the
museum of the Louvre; it is of gilt wood, and is orna-
mented with wings folded protectingly about the deceased.
An inscription found in Abydos mentions buildings erected
by him in this city. A pyramidion, mentioning the name
of his wife *Mentuhôtep*, was discovered at Qurnah. The
record of a criminal procedure against Theban tomb-robbers informs us that he was buried in the Necropolis of
Thebes. The gilt-wood sarcophagus of *Anantef* is in the
British Museum, his silver-gilt diadem is in the museum
of Leyden. *Nub-cheper-Rā Anantef* is mentioned on a
statue as the conqueror of Asiatics and Nubians, but the

texts do not give any detailed accounts of his campaigns. His tomb at Drah-abul-Neggah, opposite Thebes, was discovered by Mariette in 1860–'61. The stele found in the funereal chapel dates from his fiftieth year, so that we know he reigned fifty years, and consequently must have lived at a time when the country was tranquil. At the same place fragments of two obelisks erected b this pharaoh were found. *An āa* (the Great) is one of the kings whose tombs are mentioned in the criminal procedure above alluded to. One of the Hieratic copies of the " Book of the Dead " alleges that the one hundred and thirtieth chapter was discovered in his reign.

The Mentuhôtep kings belong to the same family with the Antef kings. *Nebhôtep Mentuhôtep* is known only from a stele found at Konosso, on which he is depicted as adoring the local divinities of that region, who " throw all peoples under his feet "—i. e., give him power over them. From this we must infer that Nebhôtep carried on wars in Nubia. Of *Rā-neb-taui Mentuhôtep* we know only that he sent an expedition to the quarries of the Wâdi Hammamât to quarry a sarcophagus for him. On this occasion he caused a great reservoir to be cut in the rock, so that the men " might not die of thirst." *Ra-neb-chepru Mentuhôtep* reigned over forty-six years, as is proved by the tombstone of a certain *Meru*, who died in the forty-sixth year of this reign. We know of him only that he quarried stone in Assuan. This pharaoh must have been a ruler of some consequence, for his name is mentioned in all of the lists of kings, and in several lists his is the only name of a king ruling before the Hyksos invasion that is mentioned.

Seānch-ka-Rā was the last king of this dynasty. A very interesting inscription, graven on the rock in the Wâdi Hammamât, relates the story of one of his expeditions. In the eighth year of his reign three thousand men, under command of *Henu*, started from Qebti, at the mouth of the valley. The expedition had a twofold object: first, to quarry stone for the monarch's tomb and sarcophagus; and, second, to visit the shores of *Pewent*—i. e., the southwest coast of Arabia and the Somâli coast on the African side of the Red Sea—on a trading expedition. *Henu* accomplished both objects successfully. · To facilitate the provisioning of so large a detachment, a number of stations was established and wells sunk along the line of march. Arrived at the quarries, one detachment of the expedition settled down to work, while the other continued its march to the sea, which it reached at about the place where Qossêr now stands. From here Henu sent out a fleet—no mention is made of the building of ships—to the shores of Pewent, awaiting their return at Qossêr. The fleet brought back all the products of this country, consisting of incense, precious stones, and other valuables. Meanwhile the stone-cutters had done their work, and the expedition returned to Egypt. This expedition is memorable in that it proves that this pharaoh was firmly determined to establish a regular trade with Pewent. The undertaking was in a certain sense a pioneer expedition, the duty of which was to survey the road from Qebti to the Red Sea, and, by the establishment of watering stations, to make it practicable. The first king of whom we know that he followed in Seānch-ka-Rā's footsteps was Amenemhāt II.

The Twelfth Dynasty (2130–1930 B. C.).—The eleventh dynasty had been a period of strife; in it Egypt had been delivered from the domination of the foreign invader, the kingdom had been reunified, and the work· of reorganizing the government had been begun. So well had the last rulers of this dynasty done their work, that *Seānch-ka-Rā* could undertake the work of opening a road through the Wâdi Hammamât, from Qebti to the Red Sea; and of laying the first foundations of a direct commercial intercourse with the coast of southwestern Arabia and the Somâli coast. To what extent the work of reorganization was completed when Amenemhāt I ascended the throne we do not know, as but few monuments of the kings immediately preceding him have come down to us. Of the times embraced by the twelfth dynasty we have, however, a fair knowledge. Though the buildings erected by the kings of this dynasty have disappeared, yet the numerous inscriptions that have been preserved in all parts of Egypt contain records of their doings. Much of our knowledge of this period we owe to the tombs discovered at Benihassan and Bersheh. But even here it is not yet possible to give details, or to fully understand all the conditions that led to the rise and the fall of this house.

Sehôtep-ab-Rā, Amenemhāt (2130–2100 B. C.).

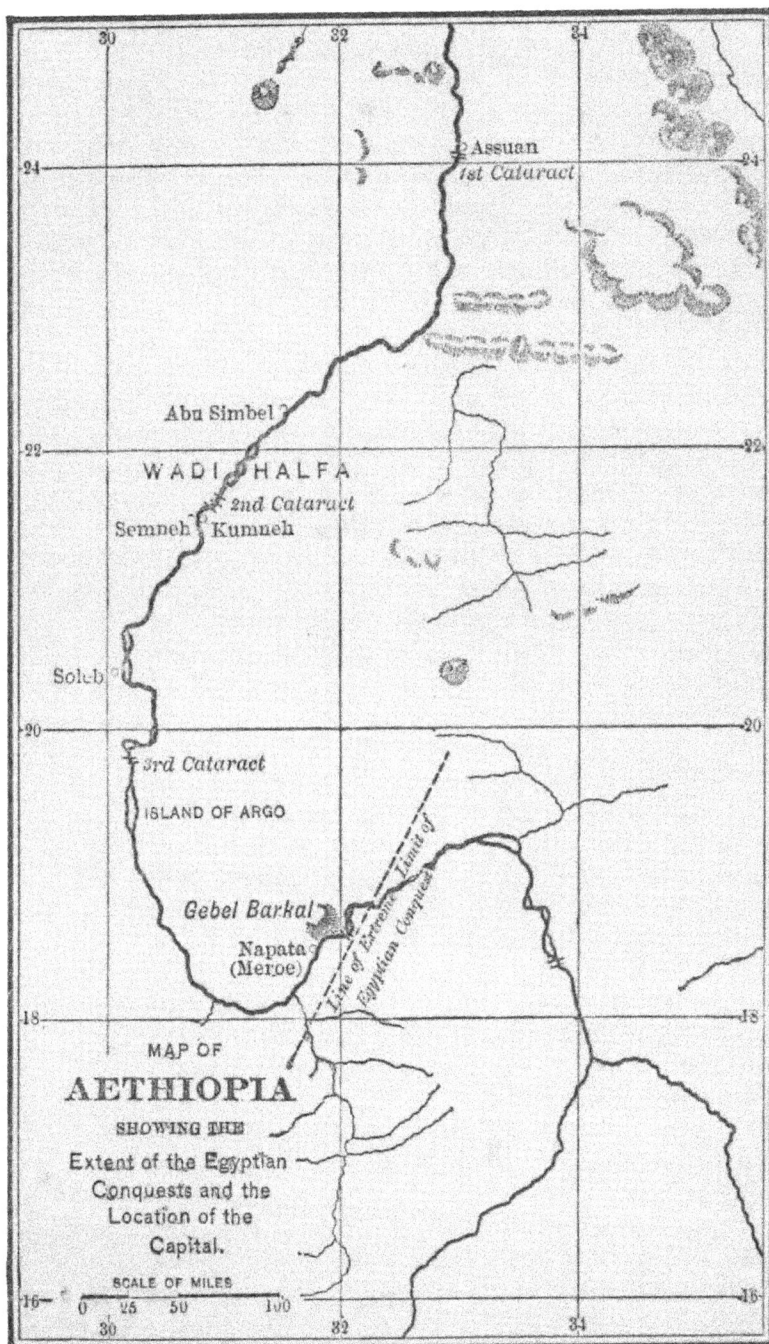

30   32   34

—24—   —24—
                              ⌖Assuan
                              1st Cataract

                Abu Simbel ?

—22—   —22—
        W A D I H A L F A
                  ⌖ 2nd Cataract
        Semneh ⌖ Kumneh

        Soleb⌖

—20—   —20—
              ⌖ 3rd Cataract

              ISLAND OF ARGO

          Gebel Barkal
          Napata
          (Meroe)

—18—   —18—

          MAP OF

        AETHIOPIA

          SHOWING THE

      Extent of the Egyptian
        Conquests and the
        Location of the
            Capital.

          SCALE OF MILES
      0   25   50   100
          30   32   34
—16—   —16—

Line of Extreme Limit of Egyptian Conquest

—About the year 2130 King Amenemhāt I ascended the throne of Egypt. What claim he had to the crown we are not told, but in all probability he was related to the last king of the preceding dynasty. The change of dynasty was not accomplished without severe internal dissensions. Several inscriptions allude to these disturbances, but give no details. The new pharaoh was equal to the occasion ; he defeated the rebels, and then set to work to reorganize his kingdom. One of his first measures was to curb the power of the nobles who had become semi-independent. The principle of heredity he dared not abolish, but he *regulated* the succession. When an old nomarchos died the king chose his successor from his heirs-at-law, and thus bound the new prince to his person. He also personally superintended a new survey of the whole country. It would seem that, during the periods of anarchy, foreign domination, and restoration, following on the decline of the Old Empire, the Egyptian kings had not possessed the leisure or the power to adjust disputes concerning boundaries which had arisen among the nobles. The stronger had preyed upon the weaker, and many a prince had seized the occasion of enlarging his domain. Amenemhāt made a tour of inspection through the country, personally hearing complaints and readjusting the boundaries. He thus succeeded in reorganizing his kingdom in a very short time, and, when order was once restored, he was the man to keep it with an iron hand. This policy enabled him early in his reign to turn his attention to foreign affairs. He marched against the Libyan tribe of the *Matjiu* and conquered them. He also warred on the Asiatic frontier against the Bedouins of the Syrian Desert. In the twenty-ninth year of his reign he led his forces into Nubia, and entirely subdued the *Ouaoua*—a tribe that had begun to give trouble. Like all the pharaohs, he was a great builder. Traces of his work have been found at Tanis, Abydos, Memphis, and Karnak. The relics of his work found at Karnak are of great importance, as they prove that the great temple of Amon was founded by this ruler. The stone needed for these buildings was quarried in the limestone quarries of Turah (*Rŏ āu*), opposite Memphis, in the diorite quarries of the Wâdi Hammamât, and in the granite quarries of Assuan. In the sixteenth Upper Egyptian nome he built a city called *Hāt-Sehôtep-ab-Rā,*

as also a fort called *Amenemhāt-Ded-Taui*. This pharaoh had in later times the reputation of being a great
sage. A papyrus, written about one thousand years after
his time, said to be a series of precepts addressed to his
son, Usertesen I, tells the story of his accession to the
throne, and relates some other events of his reign. This
interesting papyrus, which is said to have been composed
by the king himself, is preserved in the British Museum.
In the twenty-first year of his reign Amenemhāt, in all
probability with the purpose of avoiding a civil war over
the succession, appointed his son Usertesen co-regent.
This practice was imitated by most of his successors.
The pharaoh died in the thirtieth year of his reign, and
the events related and allusions made in the memoirs of
a prince of this time force on us the suspicion that he was
murdered.

Cheper - ka - Rā Usertesen (2099–2065 B. C.).
—When Usertesen I ascended the throne, about 2099
B. C., he succeeded to a mighty empire firmly united in its
various parts and presenting a bold front to its hostile
neighbors. Already as co-regent Usertesen had distinguished himself in the field, and his warlike ardor did not
abate when he sat on the throne as sole ruler. He was
compelled to take the field against the Libyan Bedouins,
whom he subdued. In the forty-third year of his reign he
invaded Nubia, and penetrated as far as the Second Cataract. Here he set up a stele, on which he enumerates
the names of eleven conquered Nubian tribes. Of these
names, nine are preserved: 1. *Huu;* 2. *Kas;* 3. (destroyed); 4. *Shemīk;* 5. *Chasaa;* 6. *Shaāt;* 7. *Asher-
kīn;* 8. *Ouaoua;* 9. *Chemer;* 10. (destroyed); 11. *Amau.*
It is very unfortunate that we have no detailed accounts of
these wars; we know only where the king warred, and
read the names of the conquered nations, but here our
knowledge ends. This pharaoh opened the copper and
malachite mines of the *Set Mefkat*—" Malachite Land,"
as the Egyptians called the Sinai peninsula. He also
quarried stone in the Wâdi Hammamât. The most important of the buildings erected by this pharaoh were, of
course, at Thebes. He built the priests' quarters at Karnak, which were restored in the reign of Ramses IX, and
had his statue placed in the temple-yard. A very fine
colossal statue of this king which was found at Tanis is

now in the Museum of Berlin. In the third year of his reign, according to the text written on a roll of leather preserved in the same museum, the pharaoh began work on the temple of *Rā* at Heliopólis. As his father was then still living, and he was merely co-regent, Amenemhāt I appears as the directing spirit, while Usertesen seems to have exercised executive functions. The temple was called *Het-chā-Sehôtepab-Rā* — i. e., "The shining temple of Amenemhāt I"—while a portion of it was named after Usertesen. The only trace left of this temple are two obelisks erected by Usertesen, one of which is still standing, while the other is fallen and in fragments. A peculiarly shaped obelisk, rounded at the apex and showing undoubted traces of the fact that it was once capped with metal, was found, broken in two, at Begīg, in the Fayoum. Owing to the fact that the Fellahīn of the region look upon it as sacred, it could not be removed. The king also built in Abydos. In his forty-second year Usertesen appointed his son Amenemhāt co-regent. Two years after he died, having ruled in all forty-four years, of which he shared ten with his father and two with his son, and ruled thirty-two alone.

Nub-ka-Rā Amenemhāt (2064-2031 B. C.) ascended the throne as sole king about 2064 B. C. He was a ruler of no special prominence, but he was well able to keep together the great kingdom left him by his father. In the twenty-eighth year of his reign this king sent an expedition under command of *Chent-chā-ouer* to Arabia and the Somâli coast (*Pewent*). The expedition was a success. This is the first time since the reign of Seānch-ka-Rā that we hear of a government expedition sent to this country. Like his father, he worked the Sinai copper-mines, and built at Sarbût el Châdem a temple to *Hathor*, who was the tutelar deity of this region. He also operated the quarries of the Wâdi Hammamât. In the thirty-second year of his reign he appointed his son Usertesen co-regent, and died three years later, having ruled in all thirty-five years—two years as co-regent of his father, thirty years alone, and three years together with his son.

Chā-cheper-Rā, Usertesen (2030-2014 B. C.).— Of Usertesen II, who came to the throne about 2030 B. C., we know but little. Almost all our knowledge of his reign is confined to what the great inscriptions in the tombs at Benihassan and Bersheh tell us of the social conditions of the time. In the first year of his reign he sent an expedition to the Wâdi Gasûs, a branch of the Wâdi Hammamât, which runs in a slanting (northeast) direction to the Red Sea. This expedition most probably went to Pewent. In the fifth year of his reign he sent an expedition under *Mentuhôtep* to Assuan, and it would seem from his inscription that the tribes dwelling about the quarries had given trouble and had been subdued. This pharaoh built at Memphis and Tanis, at which latter place a statue of his wife *Nefert* was found.

In the times of the twelfth dynasty it was a customary thing for Syrian Bedouins to cross the Egyptian border and seek permission to pasture their herds on Egyptian soil. A migration of this character which took place in the sixth year of this reign is represented on a celebrated painting found in the tomb of *Chnemhôtep*, the nomarchos of the sixteenth Upper Egyptian nome. This painting represents the arrival of thirty-seven Asiatics who came before that noble, bearing costly presents, among which was a specially valuable eye-salve, seeking his protection and asking permission to settle on his territory. The painting has become widely known through the attempted identification of the people here depicted with Abraham and his party. This attempt, however, is futile. The Bible relates that Abraham came to Egypt on a similar errand, and that his stay in this country was advantageous to him. The account of the Bible shows a good knowledge of the conditions under which such migrations were made, and is certainly based on old recollections of the race, some parts of which no doubt *did* dwell in Egypt under these conditions while they were yet in the nomadic state.

Manetho calls this king *Sesostris*, and attributes to him the conquest of the world; but as yet no monuments have been discovered that bear out this statement. As *Sesostris* is the usual designation of Ramses II with the Classical writers, it is, however, just possible that the copyists of Manetho got things slightly mixed. The king died after a reign of nineteen years, three of which he shared with his father.

Chā-ka-Rā, Usertesen (2013–1987 B. C.), who succeeded his father about 2013 B. C., is one of the greatest figures of Egyptian history. He it was that finally subdued Aethiopia. The victories of Usertesen I had placed the southern boundary of the realm at the Second Cataract. Usertesen III immediately proceeded to strengthen this frontier and make it the basis of his operations. Having defeated the hostile tribes of the region, he built two forts on opposite sides of the Nile, one at Semneh and one at Kumneh, on this cataract, and in the eighth year of his reign erected a boundary-stone warning all negroes from coming down the river on their boats unless they were bringing cattle or merchandise to market at *Heh* (Semneh) or *Aqen* (Kumneh). In the sixteenth year of his reign the pharaoh set out on his second campaign against the Nubians. He completely devastated the country, destroyed the crops, drove off the cattle, and took numerous prisoners. Despite this great victory, the Nubians were not yet completely subdued. In the nineteenth year of his reign the king was again compelled to take the field against them, and again he completely defeated them, taking large numbers of prisoners and devastating the country. After this the tribes seem to have submitted and remained tranquil, for during the rest of this epoch we hear of no new outbreaks.—The king was an active builder. We have already mentioned two of his great works. He also built in Thebes, in *Heracleopolis magna*, in Abydos, in Tanis, and in Amada. He was, moreover, the first founder of the temples on the Island of Elephantine, where he erected a temple to *Satet* and *Anuket*, two of the local deities of the region. Near the island he founded a new city, which he called *Heru-chā-ka-Rā*. It is interesting to note how posterity honored this great monarch. Almost six hundred years after the king's death, Thutmosis III erected a temple to him at Semneh, and seems to have attempted to make him a local divinity of this region. He also appears as a god in the temple of Kumneh, in that of Dôsheh, and at other places in Nubia. Usertesen died after a reign of twenty-six years.

Māt-en-Rā, Amenemhāt (1986–1942 B. C.).— About 1986 B. C., Amenemhāt III, one of Egypt's greatest pharaohs, ascended the throne. This king was not a great warrior and conqueror, but he was the projector and builder of an important work that was of far greater value to Egypt than would have been the conquest of a dozen or more of the border tribes. His fame rests on the immense reservoir he built in the western part of the twenty-first Upper Egyptian nome. This reservoir, according to all appearances, was *built* and not *dug*. A vast dam was erected inclosing a large area in this part of the country. The exact extent of the reservoir we have no means of ascertaining, nor do we know exactly what part of the district known to-day as the *Fayoum* was inclosed in its dams, some remains of which have been discovered. The object of this vast reservoir was to regulate the inundation of the Nile. It received and stored up for future use vast quantities of water. Just how this was accomplished or where the flood-gates were, or what canals led to and from the reservoir we do not know. The great work is now in ruins, and we have no description of it as it was in the days of its builder. As stated on a previous page, this work gave to the district in which it was erected the name of *Ta-she*, "Lake-land"—the modern name of the region, *Fayoum*, being derived through the Coptic *pha yôm*, from the 'ancient word *pa-yôm*, "the sea." In this reservoir Amenemhāt erected two pyramids. At Illahun, on the northern outlet of the reservoir, a city in all probability founded by the pharaoh, he built a pyramid in which he was buried. On the northeastern bank he erected the great building known as the Labyrinth, about which the Greeks tell so many stories, and which was originally a temple, dedicated either entire or in part to the crocodile-headed god *Sebak*, the head of the local pantheon of this region. The city of Crocodilopolis, the Egyptian name of which seems to have been *Shedet*, lying on the west bank of the reservoir, was the capital of *Ta-she*, and was no doubt also founded by this ruler. The Greek name of the work, Lake *Mœris*, was most probably derived from the Egyptian word *meri*, "lake." Despite the fact that the building of the reservoir and the cities lying about it must have taken up a great part of his time, Amenemhāt still was able to erect buildings elsewhere. He certainly did not forget Thebes, and we hear that he built in Abydos and Memphis. Several expeditions, one of which the king led in person, were sent to the diorite quarries of the Wâdi Hammamât. He also continued the working of the copper and malachite mines of the Sinai, and had a grotto cut into the rock at Sarbût-el-Châdem. Of interest are the notes regarding the rise of the Nile, found on the rocks at

Semneh and Kumneh, which prove that the Nile rose twenty-seven feet three inches higher at these places, during this time, than it rises to-day. Toward the close of his reign of forty-four years he appointed his son, Amenemhāt, co-regent.

Rā-mā-cheru, Amenemhāt (1941-1932 B. C.). —This pharaoh, the fourth of his name, who ascended the throne about 1941 B. C., was apparently a weak king. All we know of him is that he worked the copper-mines of the Sinai and had, like all kings of his line, the rise of the Nile carefully recorded at Semneh and Kumneh. He married his sister, *Sebak-nefru-Rā*, whom he appointed co-regent. Together they ruled about nine years. The close of the dynasty is shrouded in darkness.

6

CHAPTER IV.

THE DECLINE OF THE EGYPTIAN KINGDOM AND THE HYKSOS DOMINATION—ABOUT 1930-1530 B. C.

THIS period is one of the darkest in the history of Egypt. Very few monuments have come down to us from this epoch, and almost all we know of the entire four hundred years or more is the names of the kings and in some cases the length of the various reigns. Of some of these rulers we know from the monuments found how far their power extended, but here our knowledge ends. We know, further, that in this period the Egyptian kings were dethroned by foreign invaders coming from Asia and known to us as the Hyksos, and that these foreigners held Egypt in subjugation for many years. Who they were, and how long they remained in the country, we have no means of knowing. The only review of this period that any ancient writer has given us is that copied from Manetho :

XIII Dynasty : from Thebes, 60 kings in 453 years.

XIV Dynasty : from Chois (in the Delta), 76 kings in 484 years.

XV Dynasty : Hyksos, 6 kings in 260 years.

XVI Dynasty : Hyksos, ? kings in 251 years.

XVII Dynasty : from Thebes, ? kings in ? years.

The number of hypotheses concerning this epoch is legion, but not one is supported by facts and monuments. The times of the thirteenth and fourteenth dynasties seem to have been troublesome. The kings of the former ruled, according to Manetho, only about seven and a half years on an average, those of the latter only about six years, while the members of the first Hyksos dynasty ruled on an average forty-three and one third years. The entire period is evidently set down as too long by Manetho's copyists, who give over one hundred and forty-two kings in over fourteen hundred and forty-eight years. The monuments do not permit us to assume so great a gap in the history as five hundred and eleven years between the close of the fourteenth dynasty and the beginning of the New Empire (about 1530 B. C.). There have come down to us the genealogies of nobles who lived early in the eighteenth dynasty that after a few generations give names which certainly belonged to contemporaries of the thirteenth and fourteenth dynasties. It is very probable, if not certain, that the last kings of the fourteenth dynasty were contemporary with the earliest Hyksos kings, and we know that all of the kings of the seventeenth dynasty were contemporaries of the last Hyksos kings. If we must state the duration of this period in years, we would say that it can not have exceeded four hundred years, of which one hundred and fifty years would give about the duration of Dynasties XIII and XIV and two hundred and fifty years the duration of the Hyksos domination.

§ 1. *The Thirteenth Dynasty.*

The new dynasty, which was founded by King Rā-chu-taui, seems to have been closely connected with the twelfth. Already, at the close of the preceding dynasty, we find the crocodile god of the Fayoum, *Sebak*, in the ascendency, owing to the extensive works erected by the last kings of that dynasty in the Fayoum. Names containing that of *Sebak* as a component part begin to appear about the same time ; witness that of Queen *Sebak-nofru-Rā*. This custom has become prevalent in the new dynasty. It is further significant that two kings of this line adopted the throne-name of Amenemhāt I, *Sehôtep-ab-Rā*. A long list of kings of this house has been preserved, but of scarce a single one do we know more than the name. As above remarked, the times seem to have been troublesome and rife with insurrections and usurpations. Of *Seānch-ab-Rā*, *Amenô*, we know that he built at Karnak, two altars dedicated by him to *Amon-Rā* having been found here.

§ 2. *The Fourteenth Dynasty.*

Ransenib, the eleventh or twelfth successor of *Rā-chu-taui*, the founder of Dynasty XIII, founded a new dynasty. The greater part of his successors have left us monuments; and the fact that these monuments have been found in all parts of Egypt from Tanis to Semneh, and even far to the south of this place, proves that these pharaohs had control of the entire country, though at times they must have found it quite a difficult task to hold their own. Accordingly, we must not picture them to ourselves as exceedingly mighty monarchs. They were nothing of the kind; they merely succeeded in holding together the mighty kingdom of the twelfth dynasty. They have left us only short inscriptions and statues that are, it is true, sometimes of colossal proportions and of superior workmanship; but that could easily have been executed in a short period. Manetho states that this dynasty came originally from the town of Choïs in the Delta, but where he got this information is a mystery to us. *Sechem-chu-taui-Rā, Sebakhôtep III*, has left us several records of the rise of the Nile at Semneh and Kumneh. The sixth king of this line, *Se-mench-ka-Rā Mermenfitu*, is generally supposed to have been a usurper; but this supposition is based merely on the fact that his name, *Mermenfitu*, means "general" and is very doubtful. Of him there are extant two colossal statues that once adorned the temple of Ptah at Tanis. Both of these were later on usurped by the Hyksos king *Apepi*, and still later Ramses II put his cartouches on one of them. At the same place a third statue of this ruler was found. *Sechem-uatj-taui-Rā, Sebakhôtep IV*, was the son of a private citizen named *Mentuhôtep* and the Princess *Fu-henen-abu*, the daughter of Queen *Nenna*. It would thus seem that *Sebakhôtep IV* based his claim to the crown on his mother. *Chāseshesh-Rā Neferhôtep*, the son of a private citizen named *Hā-ānchef* and his wife *Kemāt*, was one of the mightiest of these kings, retaining the crown eleven years. The temple of Abydos was specially favored by this ruler. A long inscription found at this place relates the following story: "One day King Neferhôtep was seized with a desire to see the books of the god *Atum*, a solar deity. Receiving permission, he entered the temple library and studied them. Hereupon he resolved to restore the entire temple." A good resolution, this, and one he carried out. One of the most interesting monuments of his reign is an inscription on the rocks of Assuan, representing him and his entire family, consisting of his parents, Prince *Sa-Hathor*, Prince *Sebakhôtep*, and a relative named *Nebhôtep*. A sandstone block found at Karnak which, by the by, proves that he built here, is of great interest, as it bears on the one side the name of Neferhôtep and on the other that of *Sebakhôtep*, his son and second successor. It would seem from this that Sebakhôtep had been appointed co-regent by his father in order that his succession might be assured. A small granite statue of the king was found at Tanis. After the short reign of *Sa-Hathor*, who seems to have died soon after his accession, *Châ-nefer-Râ, Sebakhôtep V*, ascended the throne. He was a powerful monarch, who ruled over the entire land. A colossal statue of rose-colored granite representing this king, on which Ramses II afterward cut his cartouches, was found at Tanis. A second statue was found at Bubastis, and a third on the island of Argo, far south of the Second Cataract. His name is frequently found on the walls of the temple of Karnak. According to the classical authors, who call him *Chanephres*, he died of elephantiasis. *Châ-ânch-Râ, Sebakhôtep VI*, is mentioned on the walls of the temple of Karnak and on several smaller monuments. *Châ-hôtep-Râ, Sebakhôtep VII*, ruled, according to the Turin Papyrus, four years, eight months, and twenty-nine days. *Ouah-ab-Râ, Aâ-ab*, reigned ten years, eight months, and eighteen days; and *Mer-nefer-Râ, Ai*, reigned thirteen years, eight months, and eighteen days—as far as we know, longer than any other king of this dynasty. *Mer-ka-Râ, Sebak-hôtep VIII*, has left us a statue. Several important tombs at Siut date from this time. Of the remaining kings of the dynasty we know nothing. Little by little we lose grasp of the historical connection, and all that is left us is a mere list of names, with here and there the statement that a certain king ruled so and so many years. The tombs of Siut that date from this time all show that the nobles here buried were rich and powerful. They have the same value for this period as those of Benihassan have for the twelfth dynasty, but are not nearly so well preserved, and contain but few historical allusions.

§ 3. *The Hyksos Domination, about 1780–1530* B. C.

The Fifteenth Dynasty.—The fourteenth dynasty succumbed to an invasion of Asiatic Bedouins, who
gradually succeeded in driving the Egyptian kings south.
It is highly probable, however, that the pharaohs yielded
only after a long and bitter struggle. The only account
we have of the Hyksos invasion is that copied from Manetho's book by Josephus. This account is as follows :
" At the time when King Timaos ruled in Egypt, God for
unknown reasons became incensed at the Egyptians. A
people coming from the east suddenly attacked the land
and easily conquered it. The ruling class were taken
prisoners, the cities were burned down, and the temples
devastated. All the inhabitants were treated in the most
hostile and barbarous manner ; some were slain, and the
wives and children of others were sold into slavery. At
last these barbarians elected one of their own number,
named *Salatis*, king. He made Memphis his capital, levied taxes in Upper and Lower Egypt, and garrisoned a
number of towns. The strongest garrisons were laid in
the eastern forts, as he feared the Assyrians, who were at
that time very powerful, might attack Egypt. Finding in
the Saitic (mistake for Sethroitic) nome a city favorably
located, east of the Bubastic branch of the Nile, which,
owing to an old legend, was called *Avaris*, he built a great
wall around it and put in a garrison of 240,000 men. To
this city he came in the summer, partly to direct the distribution of food and pay, and partly to frighten the enemy
by constantly drilling his men. After a reign of nineteen
years he died, and the following were his successors :
Benon, who ruled forty-four years ; *Apachnas*, who ruled
thirty-six years and seven months (according to Africanus,
sixty-one years) ; *Aphobis*, also called *Apophis*, sixty-one
years ; *Annas*, fifty years and one month ; and *Asseth*, forty-
nine years and two months. These six kings were the
first rulers of the people that lived in constant strife with
the Egyptians and sought to exterminate them. The
whole people had the name of Hyksos—i. e., ' shepherd-
kings,' for *hyk* signifies in the old language ' king ' and
sos ' shepherd,' and still has this meaning in the Demotic.
Some say they were Arabs. In another copy of Manetho,
however, there is the note that the syllable *hyk* does not

signify 'king,' but that the entire word signifies 'prisoners of war.' This latter explanation seems to me," adds Josephus, "the more plausible and better in accord with ancient history."

The last note given by Josephus was certainly not found in the original work of Manetho, but was added by some later copyist, provided it be not an invention of Josephus himself. This writer's object, in quoting this passage from Manetho in his " History of the Jews," was to prove that the Hyksos and the Jews were one and the same people, and thus to demonstrate the great antiquity and nobility of the Jewish race. Now, there was one thing that bothered him. The Hyksos entered the land as conquerors, while the Jews, according to the Old Testament, entered it peacefully. Josephus, therefore, bethought himself of this not over-ingenious compromise.

On the other hand, Manetho's etymology is correct. *Heq* does mean prince, and *hyk* may well be corrupted from this word ; and *sos* certainly is a corruption of *shasu* or *shas*, which was the name commonly applied in this period to the nomads on the Asiatic frontier. I must in this connection remind the reader of the fact that the Greeks had no *q* and no *sh*, and were compelled to render the former as *k* and the latter as *s*. The only difficulty lay in the fact that *hyk* represented the singular *heq*, while the plural *hequ* would have been the proper form ; but it has been demonstrated that the form *Hyksos* is a mistake for *Hykussos*. While Manetho is right here, he has made some terrible slips in other parts of his narrative. His most glaring mistake is, that he speaks of a powerful Assyrian empire in about 1780 B. C., at a time when *Assur* was a small and unimportant town that could scarcely hold its own against its near neighbors. Even three hundred years later, Assyria was so weak that when Thutmosis III had defeated the Syrian kings, it sent him tribute. Another bad slip is the story about Avaris. Assuredly the Hyksos did not conquer Egypt in order to be able to garrison a town on the borders of the desert ! Only the bare facts of Manetho's narrative are available for historical purposes, and these are that a vast horde of Asiatic Bedouins (this is the best rendering of *Shasu*) invaded Egypt, and after a long struggle succeeded in conquering the country. What race these Bedouins belonged to we can not say, nor have we any idea of their appearance. The monuments found at Tanis and formerly attributed to them have long since been proved to belong to another epoch of Egyptian history.

Their religion was of course different from that of the Egyptians. An Egyptian text treating of the expulsion of the Hyksos states that they worshiped the god *Sutech*. This is the name applied by the Egyptians to the god of the foreigners, and is often a translation of the Semitic Ba'al. Thus the Ba'alim of the various Cheta towns are designated as *Sutechu* (plural of *Sutech*). As god of the foreign enemies of Egypt, *Sutech* is identified with *Set*, the enemy of Horus and principle of evil; and it is but natural that this god should be looked upon as the tutelar deity of the hostile foreigners. In later times, when the power of the New Empire declined, *Sutech*, as the powerful god of the mighty enemies, was considered a very potent divinity, and found many worshipers in Egypt. The names of most of the Hyksos kings are compounds of the name of the god *Set*, but some are compounds of the name *Rā*, showing that the Hyksos were to some extent influenced by Egyptian religious thought.

The Sixteenth Dynasty.—The Hyksos did not always remain uncultured barbarians, but with time began to adopt the civilization of Egypt. Egyptian officials were put in charge of the various departments; Egyptian literature, science, and art were encouraged. Under King *Aā-oueser-Rā, Apepi I*, was compiled a mathematical treatise, of which a copy, written in the twenty-third year of his reign, has come down to us. *Aā-qenen-Rā, Apepi II*, is known from several monuments. The reign, or rather death, of King *Aā-pehti-Set, Nubti*, is used as an era in an inscription of the time of Ramses II, which is dated four hundred years after King *Nubti*. This would place Nubti in the seventeenth century, somewhere between 1700 and 1630 B. C., as the inscription unfortunately does not give the year of Ramses's reign. Of the other Hyksos kings, we know the names only.

§ 4. *The Seventeenth Dynasty.—Beginning of the Struggle for Independence.*

Toward the close of the Hyksos domination there ruled in Thebes a line of kings who were, in all probability, descended from the last kings of the fourteenth or, perhaps, of the thirteenth dynasty. They are the rulers of the seventeenth dynasty who began the combat with the Hyksos. A legend preserved on a papyrus belonging to the British Museum (Sallier I) relates the story of the outbreak. King *Apepi*, the Hyksos ruler, who was an ardent worshiper of *Sutech*, sent messengers to the Egyptian king of Thebes, *Rā-seqenen Ta-āa*, bearing certain propositions regarding religious matters which *Rā-seqenen* rejected. There had also arisen misunderstandings regarding a well lying on or near the border, in regard to which no agreement could be reached. This brought on the war. *Rā-seqenen* is called throughout the story " Prince of the Southern City "—i. e., Thebes ; and it would seem from this that the Hyksos had either never reached that city, or the country had been reconquered so far north as Thebes. At all events, the Theban kings were independent rulers, and resented the Hyksos king's attempt to assert any claim of sovereignty over them ; and they boldly took up the cause of Egyptian liberty. Long years the war lasted, and the Hyksos were slowly driven north. The kings who distinguished themselves in this war were *Rā-seqenen Ta-āa · I*, *Ta-āa II*, the Great, *Ta-āa III*, the Brave, and *Kames*, the husband of Queen *Aahhôtep* and father of Aahmes I, the final liberator of Egypt. In 1881 the mummy of King Rā-seqenen was found in a shaft at Dêr-el-bahâri. An ugly gash on the head of the mummy proves that the king died a violent death. In all probability he was killed in his struggle for the liberty of his country.

CHAPTER V.

FROM THE EXPULSION OF THE HYKSOS TO THE CLOSE
OF THE EIGHTEENTH DYNASTY—ABOUT 1530–1340
B. C.—BEGINNING OF THE NEW EMPIRE.

WITH this dynasty begins the period commonly known as the *"New Empire,"* which embraces the eighteenth, nineteenth, and twentieth dynasties. The dynasty is memorable in several respects. In the first place, the first great campaigns against Asia were undertaken in this time, and Egypt was thus made a conquering power; and, in the second place, a great religious reform, which is of special interest to us moderns, was attempted by one of the rulers of this line.

§ 1. *Aahmes I.*

How long the war between the kings of Thebes and the Hyksos lasted we can not tell; but it is safe to assume that it began late in the seventeenth or early in the sixteenth century B. C. An inscription on the tomb of *Aahmes*, one of King Aahmes's admirals, gives us an account of the closing scenes of the great struggle. It would seem that the predecessors of Aahmes had driven the Hyksos into the Delta, and that they had thrown themselves into the city of *Hātouār* (Avaris), in the northeastern part of the Delta, which they strongly fortified. After several battles had been fought on land and water in the neighborhood of the city, the pharaoh laid siege to it, and, after a protracted resistance, the town finally fell into his hands. Thus, about 1530 B. C., Egypt was finally cleared of the foreign invaders that had held the land in subjugation for centuries. The fleeing Hyksos had gone to Asia, pursued by the pharaoh. Crossing the boundary, he proceeded against the town of *Sharhan*,

MAP ILLUSTRATING
Campaigns of Aahmes I.
THUTMOSIS I.
AND
THUTMOSIS III. IN ASIA.

SCALE OF MILES
0   50   100

which is mentioned, Joshua.xix, 6, as belonging to the territory allotted to the tribe of Simeon, and captured it in the fifth year of his reign. He then invaded Phœnicia and gained several victories. These successes secured the Egyptian frontier from inroads of the Asiatics for a number of years.

This was not, however, the only result of this successful war. Aahmes's Asiatic campaign had shown the Egyptians the way into Asia, and many of his successors gained their laurels in this country. The wars had also trained generals and armies, and Aahmes's successors saw to it that neither deteriorated. A new spirit had come over the once peaceful people, and army after army set out on warlike expeditions. *Amon* and *Mentu*, the great gods of Thebes, became war-gods, in whose names the kings fought their wars, and into the temples of Amon poured the lion's share of the booty won in war and the tribute wrung from conquered nations. The entire character of the wars, too, was changed by the introduction of the horse from Asia. The home of the horse was most probably the Turanian steppe. It was introduced into Egypt by the Hyksos. Horses were not used in this time as beasts of burden, but only in war and on the chase. They were not used for riding, but only to draw the two-wheeled chariots. These chariots were imported into Egypt from Syria, where chariot-building was a flourishing industry. The very word for chariot—*merkabet*—is of Semitic origin. This new arm entirely changed the character and dimensions of battles. Moreover, chariots and horses were expensive, and the charioteer required special training. These two circumstances favored the formation of standing armies, and increased the advantage the greater states had over their smaller neighbors. These facts will account for the successes the Egyptians won over the Syrian states in the ensuing centuries.

Aahmes had scarcely finished his Asiatic campaign when he was compelled to take the field against the *Chent-nefer*, a mountain tribe of Aethiopia. In a great battle this tribe was utterly routed, and the king, glad of his easy victory, was already returning home, when the news reached him that the Aethiopians had again invaded the country, and were even desecrating the temples of the gods. Rapidly returning, he fought the battle of *Tenta-āa* in northern Aethiopia, again completely routing the enemy. Not dismayed by these repeated defeats, the Aethiopians a third time returned to the attack under a leader named *Tenta-ān,* but a third time they were defeated, and this time with such frightful loss that they did not again venture to attack their successful opponents. In these wars the above-mentioned admiral, Aahmes, who had begun his career as adjutant of this king, but had rapidly earned promotion, greatly distinguished himself, and received the "gold for bravery" several times. The "gold for bravery" was a reward paid to distinguished soldiers and civilians out of the public treasury, and consisted of munificent gifts of gold in the shape of disks, bees, lions, etc. Aahmes received these gifts on seven different occasions.

There are indications in the inscription of Aahmes that the pharaoh had to put down a rebellion in the south. This rebellion probably stood in some connection with the Aethiopian wars; but we know none of the details. In fact, we never hear much of the civil wars of Egypt, of which there were no doubt many; they are always alluded to in general terms, and the details are never entered into.

Having now secured Egypt against foreign invasion, and having quelled a probably dangerous rebellion, Aahmes was free to devote the remainder of his reign to internal improvements. He ruled over twenty-two years. How much of this time was taken up by his wars we do not know. At all events, he had abundant time to strengthen his reign, and to make Thebes, his capital, the greatest city in the land. It was no easy task that was set this pharaoh. Everywhere the temples had suffered from neglect and, during the late wars, from the depredations of the Hyksos in the north and the Aethiopians in the south. Aahmes was, however, equal to the task, He immediately set to work and began the restoration and rebuilding of all the temples in the land. His own city of Thebes was the special object of his care. The city had been the capital of the land for several centuries, and already the kings of the twelfth dynasty, five hundred years and more before Aahmes's time, had laid the first foundations of its future greatness. They had laid, too, the first foundations of the great national temple of Egypt—the temple of Amon at Karnak. This temple was enlarged by our king. The city steadily grew from this time on, and in the course of a few decades became the greatest city of the land, and consequently of the then known world. The story of the rise, decline, and fall of Thebes is an integral part of Egyptian history.

When Aahmes died, after a reign of over twenty-two years, he was buried in the Theban necropolis, on the west bank of the Nile, opposite the city, at Drah-abul-Neggah. His mummy, incased in a wooden casket, was recently discovered at Dêr-el-bahâri, together with a large number of other royal mummies.

§ 2. *Amenhôtep I (Amenophis).*

Aahmes was succeeded by his son, Amenhôtep I, the early part of whose reign was shared with his mother, *Aahmes-nefert-ari.* The queen was, after her death, worshiped as a divinity, an honor accorded all kings but very few queens. Early in this reign the Aethiopians again became troublesome, and the pharaoh marched against them. He crossed the frontier, and in the battle that ensued captured the opposing general with his own hand. The victory won, the Egyptian army overran the country, and it would seem that some detachments even advanced as far as Meroë, the Aethiopian capital. The southern campaign was brought to an abrupt close by the news of trouble on the northern frontier. In a remarkably short time the king arrived at the seat of war—Libya —and defeated the enemy. This king, like his father, was frequently compelled to invade Asia, but on the whole this reign was more peaceable than the preceding one. Amenhôtep was a great builder, and continued the work of improvement and restoration begun by his father. He died after a reign of twenty-two years. His mummy was found at Dêr-el-bahâri.

§ 3. *Thutmosis I.*

The son of Amenhôtep I was a very young man when he ascended the throne, and the conquered nations sought to take advantage of this fact to regain their independence. Immediately after his accession the Aethiopians began war. The pharaoh crossed the frontier, and, after defeating the enemy in a decisive battle, overran and plundered the country, drove off the cattle, and carried large numbers of the inhabitants into slavery. This was the usual way of conducting an Aethiopian campaign; it was, as a rule, no more than a raid, made to punish the Aethiopians for a similar raid on Egyptian territory. Thutmosis varied the usual programme by hanging the body of the Aethiopian leader by the heels to the stern of the royal ship. Thutmosis now instituted a new Aethiopian policy. The configuration of the land was much the same as that of Egypt, and it was not over-difficult to introduce the Egyptian system of government in the land. Accordingly, he divided Aethiopia into a number of districts, over which he placed governors, while over the entire region he set a governor-general with the title of "Prince of Kush." What the duties of this official were is not clear. In all probability he was a sort of viceroy invested with civil and military power and responsible to the king alone. This official held a high position at the court, and was, in later times, not unfrequently a royal prince. Colonists were sent out, temples built, and forts erected and garrisoned. The chief of these forts were *Heh* (Semneh) and *Aqen* (Kumneh), which had been built by the great conqueror of Aethiopia, Usertesen III. They were no doubt greatly strengthened by Thutmosis. Aethiopia was thus secured, and even made a province of Egypt, but the mountain tribes continued to be troublesome all through Egyptian history.

Early in this reign, too, a rebellion broke out in the district of the city of Buto, in the Delta, and so serious did it become that the pharaoh was compelled to proceed against it in person. He succeeded in quelling the outbreak, and at once marched against Asia. Crossing the Arabian Desert and Palestine, he entered the land of *Rutenu* (Syria). Here an army had been drawn up to check his advance, but he defeated it with frightful slaughter and took large numbers of prisoners. He then advanced to the Euphrates River, on the banks of which he set up two stelæ to commemorate his victories and mark the boundaries of his realm. Hereupon the Egyptian army retired; and herein lay the radical fault of the Egyptian foreign policy. This fault cost them dear; for they were compelled to send army after army into Asia. In fact, the Asiatic campaigns were mostly plundering expeditions on a large

River. This town met with the usual fate. Aradus was again taken and sacked, and Tyre suffered the same fate after a short siege.

The following two years were devoted to a great campaign in Palestine. The fortress of *Anretu*, on Lake *Nesruna*, was taken and sacked after a short siege, and the entire country was overrun, as was also part of Syria. In the thirty-third year of his reign Thutmosis again invaded Syria, and this time advanced to the Euphrates River. Sailing down the stream, the pharaoh proceeded against the King of *Neharen* (Mesopotamia), who had massed his forces near his capital, *Nîī*. These forces were defeated, and Nîī was taken and sacked. Sailing still farther down the river, Thutmosis took a number of forts. He then returned to Nîī and instituted a great elephant-hunt, on which occasion a hundred and twenty of these noble animals were killed. In the following year another rebellion broke out in Syria, where three cities lying in the district of *Anaukasa* had formed a coalition. Again the pharaoh invaded the country, punished the rebels, and returned home with a long string of captives and laden with booty. In this same year one of the Aethiopian princes sent the king his daughter as a present. In the following six years only two campaigns of importance were undertaken. The first of these was against the Syrian fortress of *Areana*, in the thirty-fifth year; the second was against the fortress of *Anau kasa*, in the same country, which city had given trouble before, three years later. In the forty-first year of his reign the king set out on his last Asiatic campaign. Marching along the seacoast, he first took the fortress of *Arantu*, and then, entering Palestine, captured several cities. Entering Syria he next took the town of *Tunep*, and hereupon marched against *Qadesh*, which seems to have been the soul of the new coalition. He defeated the Cheta army before the city, which he then laid siege to. A Mesopotamian army, which made an attempt to raise the siege, was utterly routed, and left six hundred and ninety-one prisoners in the hands of the victor. Qadesh was now stormed and sacked. This ended all opposition to Egyptian rule in Asia: the backbone of the country was broken.

Thutmosis has left us long lists of names of captured cities and conquered nations containing hundreds of names;

but only very few of these can be identified with names of
cities occurring elsewhere, and we are utterly in the dark
as regards the situation of most of these cities and countries.
The extent of these conquests has been greatly exagger-
ated. On the whole, the Amanus Mountains and the
Euphrates River seem to have been the boundaries of the
conquered region.* Although the king certainly did cross
the Euphrates twice, and did defeat the armies of Mesopotamia and take Mesopotamian cities, he did not succeed
in holding these conquests. That he reached the city
of Nineveh is very doubtful. *Nii* may be the Egyptian
name of Nineveh, but in all probability it is the name of a
city lying much farther up the river on the other side from
the country of the *Cheta*; its king seems to have been
allied with the Syrian countries with which Thutmosis was
at war. It is noteworthy that the king in the thirty-third
year of his reign set up two stelæ on the banks of the
Euphrates, near Nīi, by the side of those set up his father,
Thutmosis I. The coast of Phœnicia was under Egyptian
control. Aradus, Symiria, Joppa, and Tyre submitted only
after a siege; the other cities seem to have yielded without a struggle. It was obviously to their advantage to
stand under Egyptian rule, for Egyptian rule meant Egyptian protection, and the wily Phœnician merchants soon
found that they could reap great commercial advantages
from their connection with Egypt. The Phœnician colonies in Cyprus (Eg. *Asebi*) also submitted voluntarily,
and paid tribute, though standing in no danger of invasion
from Egypt. This ready submission secured for them
great advantages—the protection of Egypt and unbroken
connection with the mother-land. As Egypt did not interfere in their internal affairs, the Phœnician cities of the
mainland and of Cyprus cheerfully paid tribute.

    The material prosperity of Egypt was greatly aug-
mented by the successes of this king, and all the tombs,
even those of the humbler citizens, give evidence of this
fact. Generals and soldiers enriched themselves in these
Asiatic campaigns as well as the pharaoh. The lion's
share of the booty and tribute, however, went to Amon,
the great god of Thebes. In the name of Amon Thutmosis had undertaken his campaigns, and with the aid of the

---

* See map.

god he had won his victories ; and in gratitude to him the
king erected the mighty buildings at Karnak, on the walls
of which he proclaimed these victories. But the other gods
were not forgotten ; in all parts of Egypt the king built,
restored, or completed temples. Of special importance
was the temple of Semneh, which was dedicated to the
deified King Usertesen III, the conqueror of Aethiopia.
In the fifty-fourth ear of his reign this mighty ruler died
and was succeeded by his son. The mummy of this king
was found in a shaft at Dêr-el-bahâri. The monarch
was a small man—the mummy is only five feet two inches
long—but with a determined cast of features, somewhat
resembling that of Napoleon I.

§ 7. *Amenhôtep II, Amenophis (1427–1422* B. C.).

One day after the death of his father, Amenhôtep II
ascended the throne. Already as crown prince he had
shown his ability in subjugating the nomadic tribes that
dwelt in the mountains between the Nile and the Red Sea,
and compelling them to pay tribute. Immediately after
his coronation the new pharaoh invaded Asia and gained
a series of brilliant victories. It seems that a new rebellion had broken out, and that the distant city of *Nii* alone
had remained loyal, for when he entered this town the inhabitants received him with demonstrations of great joy.
The campaign came to an end with the capture of the
fortress of *Akati*. His next campaign was directed against
the country of *Techsi*, in Syria, where he fought against a
mighty coalition. Seven native kings were killed, and the
land was again subdued. The bodies of the dead kings
he took with him to Egypt ; six of them he had hung up
on the walls of his capital, Thebes, and one on the walls of
Napata, as a warning to the Aethiopians. Like all rulers
of this dynasty, he was a great builder. He died after a
short reign of only five years.

§ 8. *Thutmosis IV (1421–1414* B. C.).

Of the son and successor of Amenhôtep we know little
more than that he ruled only seven years. He fought in
Aethiopia, Phœnicia, and Syria, probably quelling minor
revolts and repelling invasions of nomadic tribes. In the

first year of his reign he caused the great Sphinx of Gizeh to be freed from the sand which had accumulated about this venerable monument.

§ 9. *Amenhôtep III* (*1413–1377* B. C.).

In the fifth year of his reign, *Amenhôtep III*, the son and successor of Thutmosis IV, invaded Aethiopia, and easily subdued a number of rebellious Nubian tribes. The victory did not amount to much, but the pharaoh made a great fuss over it, having it recorded on several stelæ. This reign marked a new era in the relations with Asia. A number of tablets was recently found at Tell-el-Amarna, which contain letters addressed by Asiatic kings to kings of Egypt. A number of these is addressed to Amenhôtep III. The most interesting one is that from King *Dushratta*, of *Mitâni* (Eg. *Satarna* of *Neharen*—i. e., Mesopotamia), in which Amenhôtep is called the son-in-law of *Dushratta*. This *Dushratta* is no doubt identical with the King *Satarna* of *Neharen*, who, in the tenth year of this reign, sent Amenhôtep his daughter *Kirkipa* and three hundred and seventeen ladies for the pharaoh's harem. Although already happily wedded to Queen *Tii*, one of the most beautiful women of all antiquity, the pharaoh had no recourse but to make the princess his legitimate wife. This marriage was, in all probability, entered into after the final ratification of a treaty concluded between the two monarchs, and, in fact, the treaty concluded between Amenophis's son, Chuenaten, and Dushratta distinctly refers to this previous treaty. It is a curious fact that the letters addressed to this king and to his son are written in *Assyrian*. The king was a passionate hunter, and an inscription engraved on several scarabæi relates that in the first ten years of his reign he killed a hundred and two lions.

Like all his predecessors, Amenhôtep was a great builder. He was the builder of the celebrated temple of Amon-Râ, at Louqsor. The two celebrated " statues of Memnon," on the west bank of the river opposite Thebes, belong to this monarch. They stood originally in front of the pylon of his temple in the necropolis; but every trace of the temple has vanished. The statues were erected at his orders by the architect and sculptor *Amen-*

hôtep, the son of *Hâpi*. They are of hard red crystalline sandstone, quarried at the Djebel-el-Ahmar (Eg. *Du desher*), in the desert northeast of Memphis. The Greeks took the statues for those of the Aethiopian king Memnon, mentioned by Homer, and explained the sound produced by the northern statue as the greeting of Memnon to his mother, Eos. The explanation of this sound is very simple. The upper portion of the statue was broken, and when the sun rose the change in temperature caused the particles of stone in the crack to split, and this splitting produced a musical sound. After the statue was repaired by Septimus Severus (reigned A. D. 193-211), the sound was no longer heard.

§ 10. *Amenhôtep IV, Chuenaten (1376-1364 B. C.).*

This pharaoh is to us one of the most interesting of ancient monarchs, as the first promulgator of *monotheism*. The Egyptian people up to this time had possessed no uniform religion, but a large number of religions had existed side by side, some being recognized throughout the land, others having only local import, while one religion—that of the national capital—was the official religion of the government. At this time Thebes was the capital of the land, and the Theban religion was the government faith; consequently, the head of the Theban pantheon, *Amon*, was the official head of the national pantheon. But there had arisen in Heliopolis (Eg. *On*), the great seat of the *Râ*-religion, already in early times a movement toward a *solar monotheism*, and in Chuenaten's reign this movement was victorious. The new king was a fanatical adherent of this doctrine; he, moreover, seems to have stood entirely under the domination of the Heliopolitan priests, and gladly lent his hand to accomplish their purposes. A new official religion was accordingly proclaimed. This was a solar monotheism; the new god was, with a studied avoidance of the old names, called *Aten*, "the Solar Disk," and was proclaimed to the nation as their sole and only god. If this had signified merely a change in the *official* religion of Egypt, and not in the very inmost nature of the religion, the people would have heeded it little and gone on praying to their own *local* gods, and officially recognizing the new official head of the

8

pantheon, as they had done heretofore. But here was a complete and utter religious revolution, pronouncing *all* of the old faiths heretical and supplanting them by a faith the nature of which the people *did* not and *could* not understand. A propaganda of this character, no doubt assisted by attempts to convert the people by force, naturally led to discontent; and it was probably owing to this that the reformers graciously permitted the solar divinities *Horus, Rā, Rāharmachis,* and some few others to continue in existence, explaining them as *forms* of their new and only god *Aten.* Amon, however, was persecuted in the approved orthodox manner. Wherever he could, Amenhôtep, or, as he now called himself, *Chuenaten,* had the name of this hated divinity obliterated from the monuments, even in the names of his predecessors.

After the reformation Chuenaten left the tainted city of Thebes, the stronghold of the old Amon cult, and built himself a new capital to the north of this city, and called it *Chut-Aten,* "The Horizon of the Solar Disk." The ruins of this town, which was never completed, lie at a place called Tell-el-Amarna, and are of peculiar interest as they, together with the tombs in the necropolis of the city, give us a life-like picture of the court of this fanatical and half-crazed king. One of his peculiarities was to substitute for the conventional style of Egyptian sculpture a more realistic style. The pharaoh himself was hideously ugly, owing to a bodily deformity, and he commanded his artists henceforth to depict him in his real shape. Naturally, his wife—who seems, by the by, to have had quite a lovely face—and daughters were pictured as equally ugly, and the courtiers, as true courtiers would, aped royalty, and had themselves depicted in the likeness of their king.

Unfortunately, the reformation proved a failure, and we know but little of the new faith. Long and beautiful hymns, full of fervent devotion, addressed to Aten, have come down to us, as have also various representations of religious ceremonies. The new god is always depicted as a solar disk, the rays of which terminate in hands; but the monuments do not give us any deeper insight into the new religion.

There was in this reign no trouble with Asia. This was a result of the diplomatic negotiations begun under Amenhôtep III, and concluded by this pharaoh. Treaties of peace were concluded with *Dushratta*, of *Mitâni* (*Satarna*, King of *Neharen*, i. e., Mesopotamia), *Burna-buriash*, King of *Karduniash* (Babylonia), and *Ashuru-ballit*, King of Assyria. All these treaties contain references to former negotiations with Amenhôtep III ; they are all written in Assyrian, and are quite difficult of interpretation, though the general import of these documents can easily be given.

After a reign of only twelve years Chuenaten died, and it is not at all doubtful that he lost his life in a revolt brought on by his fanatical attempts to convert the people to his new faith by force. He had no son, but seven daughters, who were married to Egyptian nobles. Disputes over the succession immediately arose, and the country was plunged into all the horrors of a civil war.

§ 11. *The Struggle for the Succession* (*about* B. C. 1363–1340).

How long the civil war lasted we can not say, nor do we know exactly in what order the various kings that followed Chuenaten succeeded one another. In all probability the next successor of Chuenaten was Seâa-ka-Râ Sanecht, the husband of his favorite daughter, *Meraten*. He was throughout his short reign a firm adherent to the faith of his father-in-law ; but the revolution that had dethroned his father-in-law proved fatal to him also. He was deposed by the priest *Aï*, who was originally a firm adherent to the Aten-religion. Aï was a brother of one of Chuenaten's nurses, and had risen rapidly at court until he attained the position of Lord Equerry, one of the highest offices in the gift of the crown. At the time Aï dethroned *Sanecht*, the reaction was at its height, and Aï was not the man to swim against the tide. He therefore returned to the old faith and the old capital. But he had nothing outside of this to recommend him to the people, and so his apostacy availed him little. Four years after he had wrested the crown from Sanecht he was overthrown, and Ded-ânch-Amon, the husband of Chuenaten's third daughter *Anchnes-pa-Aten*, who now changed her name to *Anchnes-Amon*, ascended the throne. Like his predecessor, he was an apostate from the Aten-religion, but this policy availed him as little as it had his antagonist. After a reign of only four years he lost his throne and his life, and with him the last of Chuenaten's heirs sank into the grave. After his death the confusion became worse than ever. King after king ascended the throne, but they all fell before they had tightened their grasp on the reins of state. How long this state of affairs lasted we can not say, but in our opinion the entire period from the death of Chuenaten to the end of the civil war can not have embraced less than about twenty or twenty-five years. At length *Hor-em-heb*, who was in some way, possibly through his wife, *Mut-netjem*, connected with the royal family, succeeded in restoring order, and with him begins the nineteenth dynasty.

ASIA

MINOR

AMANUS Mts.

KARKEMISH

NEHEREN

Euphrates R.

Delicious R.

HETA

TUNEP (?)

Charbu (Aleppo)

QADESH (?)

SHABTUN (?)

Orontes R. (Aruna)

MEDITERRANEAN SEA

CYPRUS

ARADUS

LEBANON

CITY AND RIVER BERYTOS

Sidon

TYRE (TSAR)

QADESH

AKKA

Chal

RUT

ASQALON

GAZA

PELUSIUM

Raphia

EGYPT

DESERT
THE SHASU

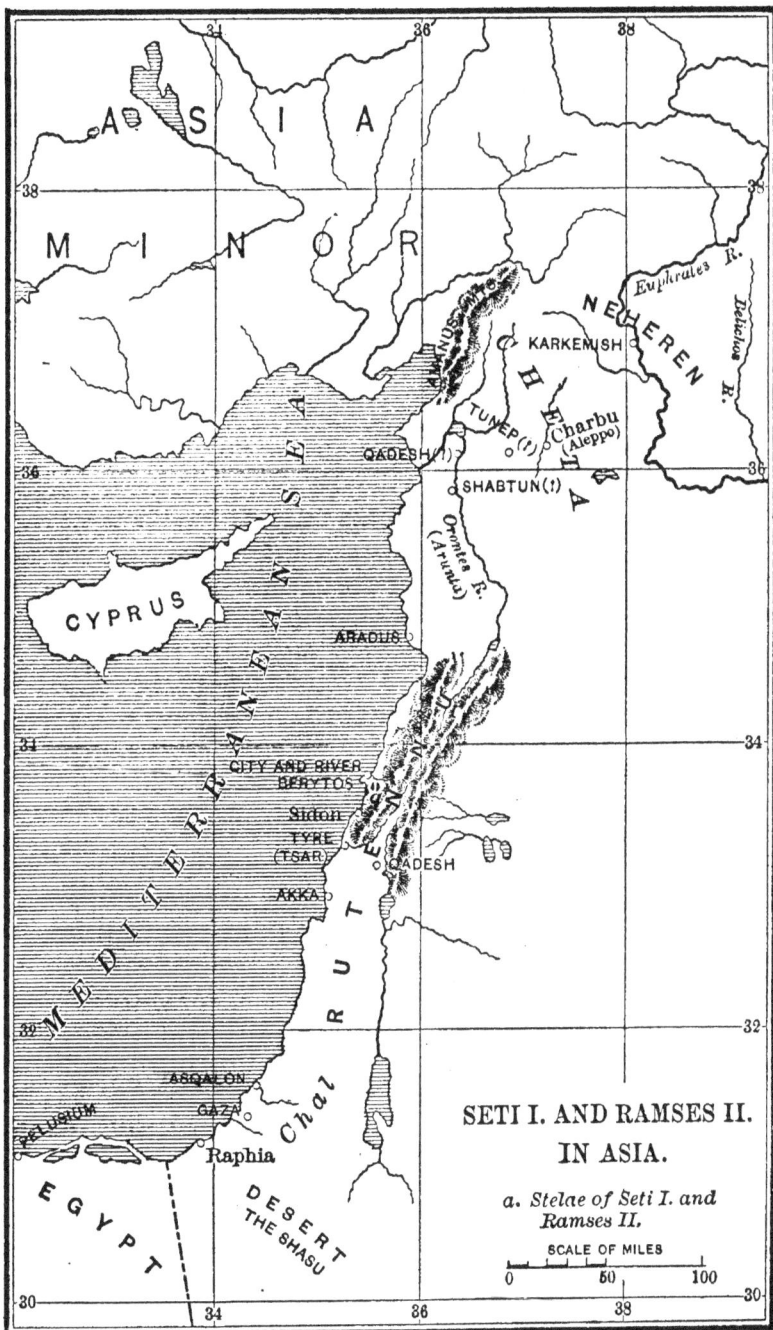

SETI I. AND RAMSES II.
IN ASIA.

a. Stelae of Seti I. and
Ramses II.

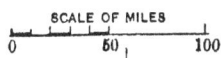

SCALE OF MILES

0   50   100

CHAPTER VI.

THE NINETEENTH DYNASTY—ABOUT 1330–1180 B. C.

§ 1. *Hor-em-heb (1340–1320 B. C.).*

ABOUT 1340 B. C. Hor-em-heb succeeded in restoring order in the kingdom. His accession to the throne marks a new era in Egyptian history, that of the nineteenth dynasty, in which Egypt, though its armies no longer marched to the Euphrates and became the terror of the Mesopotamian rulers, yet succeeded in making a part of Asia an integral part of its empire. The preceding dynasty had produced great conquerors who stand unrivaled in the annals of the land of *Qêmet.* This dynasty produced rulers who were great warriors, and, but for events which had occurred in Asia during the latter part of Dynasty XVIII, would have equaled the two great Thutmoses in extent of conquests, and who were besides great organizers. How they succeeded in incorporating Palestine, Phœnicia, and southern Syria in the kingdom we shall presently see. The great mistake of these rulers was that they little by little substituted Libyan mercenaries for the national armies that had hitherto been the sole reliance of Egypt, and we shall have occasion to trace the grave results of this mistake.

A long inscription on a statue of Hor-em-heb, preserved in Turin, gives us an account of his early life and relates how he came to the throne. He was brought up in the city of *Hat-suten*, and already in his early youth was highly honored. He was a member of the family of Thutmosis III, whom he calls the father of his father—i. e., his ancestor. When he was still a very young man the ruling pharaoh, whose name is not mentioned, appointed him to a high position in the eighteenth Upper Egyptian nome (*Saped*), which was his home. As he made a good record in this position he was made *aden* (i. e., general), and in this position he received the tributes of the foreign princes and all the princes had to bow down before him. After he had held this position for a number of years and had shown great ability, he was appointed nomarchos of *Saped.* This position he held when, as the text puts it, Horus and Amon decided to place him on the throne. Hor-em-heb certainly had a good right to the succession, being a lineal descendant of Thutmosis III ; but his chief claim lay in the fact that he had succeeded in triumphing over all the usurpers that had arisen after the death of the last pharaoh of Chuenaten's line. On the close of the civil war he proceeded to Thebes, where he married the royal princess *Mut-netjem* and was .crowned king. His campaigns were chiefly in the south, where he put down a number of rebellious Nubian tribes. We also know that he conducted several campaigns in the north with the usual success. It would seem, too, that the connections with southern Arabia and the Somâli coast were kept up, for the inscriptions mention the tribute of the Prince of *Pewent.* Hor-em-heb tells us that he restored the temples of the land from the Delta to Nubia and increased the numbers of their slaves and the amounts of the sacrificial offerings. Of the temples, those of Thebes, On-Heliopolis, and Memphis were specially favored. Hor-em-heb died after a reign of about twenty years.

§ 2. *Ramses I (1319–1317* B. C.).

Very little is known of Hor-em-heb's son and successor, Ramses. He made several raids into Nubia, and shortly before his death appointed his son, Seti, co-regent. He died after a reign of only two years. His mummy was among those found at Dêr-el-bahâri.

§ 3. *Seti I (1316–1289* B. C.).

The son and successor of Ramses I was one of the greatest and most warlike of all the Egyptian kings. Already in the first year of his reign he was compelled to invade Asia. Starting from the *Chetem*—i. e., fort of *Tjar,* which lay on the fresh-water canal that formed the eastern boundary-line of Egypt—he first attacked and easily defeated the *Shasu*—i. e., the nomadic tribes dwelling in the Arabian Desert—and then entered Canaan, defeated the inhabitants, took their capital, and erected and garrisoned forts and dug wells in the conquered country. It is evident that the pharaoh desired to hold the land permanently, and thus to secure Egypt against all further inroads from Asia. This rapid success of the Egyptian army spread terror over all Syria, and the Syrian princes submitted peaceably and paid tribute. Several strongly fortified towns, however, held out and had to be taken by force of arms. Among these were *Qadesh,* a city of the Amorites (in the district allotted to the tribe of Naphtali), that must not be confounded with Qadesh on the Orontes, the capital of the Cheta, and the fortress of *Jenuam.* Seeing these Egyptian successes, *Mautenouer,* the king of the Cheta, naturally thinking he would be attacked next, determined to take a hand in the game. He was defeated, but Seti gained no permanent advantage over him. If we possessed the monuments of this Cheta king, we certainly would read of victories gained over the Egyptians. Seti now returned home. At *Tjar* he was met by a procession of priests and nobles, who conducted him to Thebes in triumphal procession. The successes of this pharaoh must not be overestimated. All he succeeded in doing was to conquer the land lying between the Egyptian and the Cheta frontier. The petty sovereigns of southern Syria fell an easy prey to him, but the mighty Cheta king succeeded in checking his advance. The "lists" of "conquered" lands and cities are very unreliable, many of the names having been copied from the lists of Thutmosis III.

In the later years of his reign Seti was compelled to march against the *Tehenu*—i. e., the Libyans, who had again begun to make inroads on the western frontier. The Libyan tribes, who were savage and warlike, had for centuries almost constantly been at war with Egypt, and, though at first easily defeated, had in the course of time become very dangerous foes. In this reign they began a series of invasions which were repelled only with great difficulty. Seti was compelled to defeat them again and again before he succeeded in subduing them for the time being. These tribes soon assumed the same position as regards Egypt that the German tribes in later times held as regards the Roman Empire. They began as enemies and invaders, and with time, finding it profitable to serve the pharaoh, entered the Egyptian service as mercenaries. These mercenaries soon supplanted the native troops, and in several centuries gained such controlling influence that, some four hundred years after *Seti's* time, their commander-in-chief, *Sheshonq*, could grasp the scepter and ascend the throne of the pharaohs. The Tehenu tribes that entered the Egyptian service in this and the following reigns were the *Mashawasha* and the *Qahaq*. In connection with these tribes there appears now for the first time the tribe of the *Shardana*. Large bodies of these Shardana entered the service of Egypt under Ramses II, and a poem celebrating this monarch's victory over the Cheta states that they were originally prisoners of war. The armament of these men was peculiar ; they carried small round shields or bucklers and a long, sharp-pointed lance, and wore helmets with a round ball on top. They also had full beards, while the Egyptian soldiers wore no beards at all. In later times they are called "people of the sea." Their home must consequently have been some coast district or island of the Mediterranean. We have no reason whatsoever to identify them with the Sardinians. In all probability they were a tribe that dwelt on the northern coast of Africa.

The architectural activity of this ruler was confined chiefly to Thebes, where he built at the temple of Amon-Rā at Karnak. Here he began the magnificent hypostyle, which was completed by his son and successor. In the necropolis of Thebes, on the west bank of the Nile, he restored two funereal temples, that of Mā-ka-Rā at Dêr-el-bahâri, and that of Thutmosis III at Medinet-Hâbu. He also began a funereal temple dedicated to his father, Ramses I, at Abd-el-Qurnah, which was completed by Ramses II, who dedicated it to Seti, in conjunction with Ramses I. The king also restored temples in all parts of Egypt. The mines of the *Set Mafkat*—i. e., "Malachite Region," as the Egyptians called the Sinai—he held and operated. The quarries in Egypt proper were, of course, in full operation, and the gold-mines of Aethiopia were worked. Of these gold-mines there has been preserved, in a Turin papyrus, a map which, though crudely drawn, is easily intelligible—the oldest map extant.

Before his death Seti appointed his young son Ramses co-regent, but this appointment was merely nominal. Ramses certainly never exercised the functions of this office. He himself conceived it in this spirit, never dating his reign from his appointment, as the kings of the twelfth dynasty had done, but from his actual accession to the throne as sole ruler. Seti died after a reign of about twenty-seven years. The mummy of this ruler was found in a shaft at Dêr-el-bahâri, where it had been hid to pro- tect it against the tomb-robbers that invested the necrop- olis in the times of the priest-kings of Dynasty XXI. The features are strongly marked, and give evidence of great mental vigor and strength of will.

§ 4. *Ramses II (1288–1221* B. C.).

This king has long been overestimated by those who followed Greek tradition in Egyptian history. That this tradition is utterly untrustworthy has been pointed out in the introduction, and its utter worthlessness is here glar- ingly illustrated. The Greeks called this king *Sesostris,* and made him the representative of Egyptian greatness. The *name* of Sesostris is undoubtedly authentic, being a corruption of *Sesetsu*—a name applied to this king in a critical letter written either in his reign or shortly after- ward. He has been declared the greatest of all the pha- raohs, while in reality he is to be placed after several others. Of all the greatest was undoubtedly Thutmosis III ; next after him we can place his father, Thutmosis I ; then come Usertesen III, the conqueror of Aethiopia, and Seti I, who conquered Libya and prepared the way for Ramses II in Asia.

We give now a brief summary of the Greek accounts of this king, and the reader can then himself compare them with the authentic history gleaned from the monu- ments of this reign, which, with the exception of the very suspicious "lists" of "conquered nations," are entirely trustworthy. Herodotus and Diodorus Siculus are the principal sources for the Sesostris legend. According to them, Sesostris was educated together with all boys born on the same day with himself. While yet crown prince he was sent against the Aethiopians, and subdued their en- tire country ; then he marched against Libya, and conquered the greater part of that country. His father dying soon after, he determined to conquer the world. Raising an army of six hundred thousand infantry, twenty-four thousand cavalry, and twenty-seven thousand chariots, he put them under command of the seventeen hundred boys educated together with him. This vast army first marched against Aethiopia (1), and, conquering the entire country, levied a tribute of gold, ebony, and ivory. (Why conquer Aethiopia, which, according to the same authority, he had already conquered?) He then fitted out a fleet of four hundred sail, the first (1) Egyptian fleet, and, penetrating to the land where the cinnamon grows and the Straits of Bab-el-Mandeb, conquered the land of the Ichthyophagoi, and erected stelæ there. Then he crossed to Arabia and overran that country and the Asiatic coasts as far as India. In proof of this, they state that up to their time there were to be seen in that country many " ramparts of Sesostris," as well as numerous imitations of Egyptian temples. His land-forces crossed the Ganges and conquered India. He next overran the country of the Scythians up to the Tanaïs River (the modern *Don River!*). Here a part of his troops remained, and from them are descended the Colchoi. According to Pliny's version, however, Sesostris did not succeed in invading the country, but was defeated by Saulaces, King of Colchis. The king next entered Europe, and overran Thrace. Here his army was almost entirely broken up by hardships and starvation. At length, after nine years of continued warfare, he returned home laden with booty. In all of the conquered lands Sesostris set up stelæ. Some of these monuments alleged to have been erected by him were shown to Herodotus in Ionia and Syria. Manetho relates that, when Sesostris set out on his campaigns, he had appointed his brother Harmaïs regent during his absence. After the king's return Harmaïs revolted, but was defeated at Pelusium.

The Egyptian account differs materially from this. In Libya, Ramses fought only as crown prince under his father's leadership. The monuments do, indeed, mention campaigns in Aethiopia, but these were most probably directed only against the mountain tribes that made constant inroads on the civilized portion of Aethiopia. The country proper was an integral part of Egypt and had been so for centuries, and it was entirely unnecessary to reconquer it. The great seat of the war in this reign was Asia. In the second year of his reign the pharaoh started on his first campaign in this region. It would seem that disturbances had occurred in Palestine and the land of the Amorites, and that this campaign was necessary to restore order. Several cities had to be taken, but, on the whole, the restoration of Egyptian supremacy in the countries recently so severely visited by Seti I can not have been an over-difficult task. As usual, it seems that the fortresses alone offered any resistance, and after they had fallen the rest of the country submitted peaceably. At the close of this campaign Ramses erected a stele on the banks of the Naher-el-Kaleb, north of Beyrout. His second campaign, on which he set out in the fifth year of his reign, after careful preparation, was directed against the Cheta, the old enemies of Thutmosis III and Seti I.

It may be well here to give a brief sketch of the rise of this people. There were two peoples named Cheta, one in Canaan and one dwelling between the Orontes and the Euphrates. The latter is the people we refer to here. Already in the time of Thutmosis III they seem to have been an important and influential nation. The Cheta were the soul of the last great coalition formed against this pharaoh, but in these early times Egypt still proved the master. After the death of Amenhôtep III, the Egyptians were too much occupied with internal affairs to interfere in Syria, and in the time between the death of this · ruler and the accession of Seti I falls the rise of the Cheta. Of the combats in which they gained this ascendency we know nothing; but it would seem that their kings *Sapalel* and *Marusar*, who preceded *Mautenouer*, the contemporary of Seti, had succeeded in gaining the ascendency over all the states of northern Syria (the *Rutenu heru* " Upper Rutenu " of the Egyptians), northern Mesopotamia, and of that portion of Asia lying north of their domain. We do not, however, know whether they merely stood at the head of a confederacy composed of these states, or had really conquered them. When Seti I invaded Asia, *Mautenouer* felt sufficiently strong to oppose him, and, though at first defeated, succeeded in checking his advance. This success naturally increased the prestige of the Cheta, and when Ramses II attacked them they seem to have been able to call to their aid all the peoples of northern Syria and northern Mesopotamia and some of the peoples of Asia Minor. The forces of this mighty coalition were massed in front of *Qadesh*, the Cheta capital, where they awaited the Egyptian advance. Led by treacherous guides, the advance guard of the Egyptian army, which was under the personal command of the king, fell into an ambuscade near Qadesh and were all but annihilated. They were, however, rallied by Ramses, whose personal prowess, as he tells us, alone turned the tide of battle; and when the rest of the army, which had been hastily summoned, arrived on the battle-field they were just in time to join in the pursuit of the fleeing foe. The enemy were driven into the Orontes River (Eg. *Arunta*), and suffered terrible losses; one of their generals, the Prince of *Chaleb* (Aleppo), was almost drowned. Again and again Ramses reverts to this victory; the poem and the representations commemorative of it he had inscribed on the walls of several temples. Undoubtedly it was an act of great personal bravery, and the pharaoh had a right to be proud of it; but the victory was fruitless. Qadesh was not taken, and if Ramses says that Mautenouer had turned about and adored him, this can refer only to negotiations concerning an armistice. At all events, the war went on as before, and evidently with wavering success, though we hear but little of its further course. Once we find the pharaoh fighting far north, in the region of *Tunep* in *Neharen* (Mesopotamia), but how he came there we do not know. He did not retain this advanced position long, however, but was driven back, for in the eighth year of his reign he fought in Palestine, taking the towns of *Merom*, *Karpu* in the region of *Bet Anat*, and *Dapur* in the country of the Amorites. He also took the town of *Shapur*, and finally reconquered *Asqarun* (Asqalon) which had thrown off the yoke of Egypt. During this war Mautenouer died, and *Chetasar* succeeded him. The Cheta war was finally closed in the twenty-first year of Ramses's reign by a treaty of peace and alliance. This treaty proves that perfect equality existed between the two nations. Both kings bound themselves to keep the peace and be good and faithful allies. The treaty refers to one in force in the times of Sapalel and Mautenouer, concluded possibly with Seti I or one of his two predecessors. It expressly states the obligation of either king to come to the assistance of the other if so required. It further defines the obligation of either king to return refugees. Thus was concluded the first treaty of peace and alliance the full text of which has come down to us. That treaties had been concluded between the kings of Egypt and the Mesopotamian rulers we have seen in the preceding chapter. To strengthen this treaty Ramses married the oldest daughter of Chetasar, acknowledging her as his legitimate wife and queen, the princess adopting the Egyptian name *Māt-nefru-Rā*. Thirteen years later Chetasar, accompanied by the Prince of Qedi, paid his royal son-in-law a visit. The terms of the treaty seem to have been strictly kept by both countries, as they were weary of a war that drained their resources and brought no result to either. Of the boundary between the two nations nothing is said in the treaty; but it would seem probable that Egypt retained Phœnicia, Palestine, and southern Syria, while the Cheta were free to extend their domain northward. The Cheta made good use of their opportunities. All through Asia Minor and as far north as Smyrna we meet with monuments that were erected by this people.

Ramses could not extend his sway any further than the boundaries of the Cheta. He now set to work to secure the conquered country. In all parts of Palestine and southern Syria forts were erected and garrisoned, and it would even seem that special officers rode through the land on tours of inspection. The power of Egypt had greatly weakened, and she was no longer what she had been three centuries earlier. The "lists" of "conquered lands" which this pharaoh had inscribed on the temple walls are utterly unreliable, being copied in great part from those of Thutmosis III. Thus he mentions as conquered, among others, *Assur* (Assyria) and *Sangar* (Chaldea), countries with which this pharaoh had no relations whatsoever.

That a very active commercial intercourse between Egypt and Asia was brought about by the new relations between Egypt and the Asiatic nations is self-evident. Egypt powerfully influenced Asia, and was powerfully influenced in return. Syrian divinities, *Ba'al* and *Astarte*, were taken into the Egyptian pantheon. *Set-Sutech*, who to the Egyptians represented the tutelar divinity of the foreigners, gained greatly in prestige, owing to the successes of these same foreigners. But the chief influence was on the language. The influx of Semitic words into the Egyptian at this time is something wonderful to behold. It must have been considered elegant and a proof of great learning to larder one's writings with these foreign words and phrases, for some of the texts of this period teem with them.

The peace which closed the Asiatic war in the twenty-first year of Ramses's reign left the pharaoh forty-six years to devote to internal improvements. The king directed his attention chiefly to building, and there is scarce a town in all Egypt in which he did not build, complete, or restore temples. But, despite this great activity, he does not seem to have been thoroughly satisfied with his work, for he *usurped* many temples erected by his predecessors. The usurpation of monuments was a common practice in ancient Egypt. The usurper proceeded in a very simple manner. He erased the name of the real builder and substituted his own for it, thus making it appear as if the monument in question owed its existence to him. This had been done before Ramses's time, but none of his predecessors possessed the same finesse in this class of work. He thus succeeded in arrogating to himself many temples that had been built years, and sometimes centuries, before his time; and it is often owing only to the fact that the men charged with the work did it very slovenly, and left the name of the real builder standing in some obscure corner, that we are enabled to discover the imposition,

Tanis, a city lying near the northeastern boundary of Egypt, shared with Thebes the honor of being the residence of the pharaoh. The various departments of the government were located at the latter city, but Tanis offered Ramses unrivaled facilities as a basis of operations for his Asiatic campaigns. A king who spent so many years warring in Asia would naturally find it of great advantage to fix his residence at a place so near the frontier. Tanis thus owes the larger part of its glory and prosperity to this pharaoh. He it was that built the vast granite temple. As many as fourteen obelisks and several statues of the king have been found here. Memphis also came in for a share of the king's favor; it was made one of his residences, and its temple of *Ptah* was greatly enlarged. But the great city of this reign was Thebes, of which we may well here give a brief sketch. This city, the Egyptian name of which was *Oueset*, was situated on the east bank of the Nile, its site being still marked by the ruins of the great temples of Karnak and Louqsor, both of which were dedicated to *Amon-Rā*. Between these two temples lay the city proper. The temple of Karnak had its own names; one of these was *Apet*, the other *Nes-taui*, "Throne of Both Lands (i. e., Egypt)." On the west bank of the river lay the necropolis, or cemetery of Thebes, in which its kings, courtiers, and citizens lie buried. The rulers of the Middle Empire were interred in low pyramids built on the plain, those of the New Empire were interred in tombs hewn into the living rock of the hills that skirt the valley of the Nile on the west. The temples dedicated to the cult of the pharaohs of this latter period were built in the valley—thus a long row of funereal temples extends through this plain: the temple of Dêr-el-bahâri, built by Mā-ka-Rā; that of Ramses I and Seti I at Qurnah; the Ramesseum, built by Ramses II; the temples of Thutmosis III and Ramses III at Medînet Habu, and many others. This district was devoted to the use of the dead and of those who cared for them. Masons, carpenters, embalmers, and laborers of every description connected with what the French call "*les pompes funèbres*" had their homes here. In this necropolis Ramses. was very busy. He first completed the funereal temple at Qurnah begun by his father, and then erected the wonderful Ramesseum—a temple dedicated to Amon-Rā, and commemorative of the pharaoh's victories. On the east bank of the river he completed the wonderful hypostile of Karnak which his father had begun, and otherwise improved and decorated the main building, besides erecting a building south of the pond belonging to the temple inclosure, and a pretty extensive temple east of the great temple. This pharaoh was especially partial to grotto-temples, of which he built quite a number—e. g., at Bêt Wally, Geref Hussein, Wâdi Sebua, and Abusimbel. The last-mentioned temple was the best of this class. It is the largest and most beautiful grotto ever cut from the living rock by the hand of man.

The classical authors, Strabo, Pliny, and others, ascribe to Sesostris the beginning of a canal connecting the Nile with the Red Sea, which Necho is said to have continued and Darius to have completed. The canal from Cairo to Suez was afterwards again opened by Amru, the Mohammedan conqueror of Egypt, but, one hundred and forty years later, it was again closed by order of the caliph Abu-Djar-el-Mansur. In fact, there existed already in the times of Seti I a canal which, starting from the Nile, near Memphis, ran through the Wâdi Tumilât to Lake Timseh, and thence to the Rèd Sea. This' canal is represented for the first time in an inscription of Seti I, where the return of that conqueror from his Asiatic campaign is depicted. It is pictured as full of fishes and crocodiles. The canal bears the unassuming name of *demat* "canal." A bridge led over it near the *Chetem* (fort) of *Tjar* that covered this part of the frontier. When this canal was dug we can not say to a certainty. It existed in the time of King Seti I, and may have been dug by him, but it may just as well be considerably older. It was dug originally either for purposes of irrigation or as a defense against the Asiatic Bedouins. We scarcely think that it served any commercial purposes in these early times. The canal is frequently mentioned by foreigners. Thus, the Bible mentions it as the "Brook of Egypt" (*Nahal Mizra'im*), Numbers xxxiv, 5; Joshua xv, 4; Isaiah xxvii, etc.; and in the Assyrian inscriptions it is called "the brook (*Nahal*) where there is no rivet (*Nâru*)," because it was not a natural but an artificial water-way. It is considered by these texts as the boundary-line of Egypt.

The pharaoh died in the sixty-eighth year of his reign, having previously appointed his fourteenth son, *Mer-en-Ptah*, co-regent. A word about the monarch's family may here be in place. He had several legitimate wives and many concubines. Consequently he could also boast of a large number of children. One list mentions one hundred and sixty-two of these by name—one hundred and eleven sons and fifty-one daughters. The mummy of the king was found at Dêr-el-bahâri. It shows a striking resemblance to the beautiful statue of the king preserved in the Museum of Turin. Ramses must have been in his younger days quite a handsome man, and even in old age his features preserved a determined cast.

§ 5. *Mer-en-Ptah* (*1220-1212* B. C.).

About 1220 B. C. the last great ruler of this line ascended the throne. His history is not over-eventful. The empire was at peace with the world. In the south the Egyptians held as much of Aethiopia and Nubia as practicable, their only object being to control the Nubian gold-mines and to secure the southern frontier against invasion. In Asia the advance of the Egyptian arms had received a decided check at the hands of the Cheta, and the treaty of peace and alliance concluded in the twenty-first year of the preceding reign had put an end to all chance of war in that quarter. Canaan, Palestine, Phœnicia, southern Syria, and the Sinai, were secure. The last-named country had been under Egyptian control for several thousand years, and the others were secured by numerous forts established by Seti I, Ramses II, and Mer-en-Ptah. With *Pewent* there never had been war and there was no chance of war now, as the commercial relations between the two countries continued profitable to both, and would only have been disturbed by a war. There was only one quarter from which a war could threaten and that was Libya. We have seen that the Libyans had frequently given trouble before, but that the campaign of Seti I had effectually checked them and had put a stop to their inroads for a long while. After this campaign we find that many Libyans entered the service of Seti I and Ramses II. It is hardly credible that they remained in the service after Ramses's wars were over. In all probability they returned home and told their countrymen of the wealth of Egypt and of the immense booty to be won there. Returning from successful campaigns they no doubt brought home what seemed to them great riches, and this aroused the greed of their countrymen. Ramses himself they dared not attack, but after his death they prepared to invade the land. Numerous Libyan tribes from the sea-coast and the interior—the *Lebu, Qahaq, Mashawasha, Akawasha, Turasha, Reku, Shardana,* and *Shereshka*—combined their forces with those of the frontier tribes, and, under the command of King

Maroï, the son of *Didi*, entered the western Delta in the fifth year of the new reign and advanced, plundering the country, as far as *Per Bairo* (Byblos, south of Bubastis). It was their evident intention to settle here and, if need be, to purchase the right to settle here with their blood. King Mer-en-Ptah was notified of this invasion, but he hesitated to take active measures. At last he got an army together, but was deterred from accompanying it by a dream. Meanwhile the enemy had advanced to *Per-Aru-Shepses*, a town near Heliopolis, which city their forces now threatened. At this place the Egyptian army met them, and in the battle that ensued completely routed and almost annihilated their forces. The Egyptians then plundered and burned down the fortified camp of the enemy. This victory left in the hands of the Egyptian army vast amounts of booty and a great number of prisoners. Mer-en-Ptah was a great builder. On the Egypto-Syriac frontier he erected two forts and continued the work begun by his predecessors at Thebes, Tanis, and other places. He died after a short reign of only eight years.

§ 6. *Close of the Nineteenth Dynasty (1211–1180* B. C.).

Seti II (1211–1209 B. C.), a son of Mer-en-Ptah, succeeded his father on the throne. Inscriptions and papyri of his reign are constantly bragging about his great victories, but not one of these is ever specially mentioned, nor do we know of any campaigns of this king. Evidently these laudatory hymns are mere pieces of meaningless flattery. He died after a reign of only two years. A period of anarchy followed on his death, during which several usurpers succeeded in gaining the ascendency for a short period. Of these monarchs we know only a few. *Amon-meses* and *Sa-Ptah, Mer-en-Ptah II*, were in later times regarded as illegitimate. Undoubtedly they were usurpers. A Syrian, *Arsu* by name, succeeded in making himself king for a short while, but whether he came to the front as leader of one of the hostile factions or was an invader we do not know. At last *Set-necht*, the founder of Dynasty XX and father of Ramses III, succeeded in restoring order about 1180 B. C. or perhaps a few years earlier.

CHAPTER VII.

THE CLOSE OF THE NEW EMPIRE AND THE PERIOD OF DECLINE—DYNASTIES XX, XXI, AND XXII—ABOUT 1180–800 B. C.

§ 1. *The Twentieth Dynasty and Close of the New Empire* (1180–1050 B. C.).

WITH this dynasty closes the period called the "New Empire," and begins the period of decline. The epoch known as the New Empire had begun auspiciously, and for several centuries the pharaohs of the eighteenth and nineteenth dynasties had succeeded in making and keeping Egypt the first power of the then known world. At the close of each dynasty there had occurred periods of anarchy, which were, however, of short duration, and entailed no serious consequences. The kings had, nevertheless, made a number of serious blunders, and the effects of these blunders began to show themselves in this period. The first of these was the great power which had been given the priests of Amon-Rā after the suppression of the reform movement. We have seen how the booty won in the Asiatic wars poured chiefly into the coffers of Amon-Rā. The moneys paid into his treasury were managed by the priesthood—a fact that is very significant. This priesthood was responsible apparently only to itself, and consequently vastly enriched itself. Add to the power of great wealth the control of vast estates and consequently an immense patronage, and the enormous influence the priesthood generally has over the masses, and you can readily see that sooner or later this priesthood must become very dangerous to the state. In this dynasty there must be added yet another factor—the vast influence the clergy gained over the weak and incompetent kings that ruled after Ramses III. It is no wonder, then, that they should finally succeed in snatching the scepter from the weak hands of the last Ramses. The second serious blunder was their Libyan policy, which we have outlined in Chapter VI, § 3.

Set-necht ruled only a very short while, but he appointed his son, Ramses, co-regent shortly before he died.

Ramses III (1180–1148 B. C)., the *Rhampsinitos* of the classical authors, ascended the throne about 1180 B. C. This pharaoh anxiously imitated Ramses II, even giving his sons the same names as those borne by the sons of his great predecessor, and appointing them to the same offices the latter had held. He was not, however, the equal of Ramses II in war, though he almost excelled him in braggadocio. The "lists of conquered lands" are just as untrustworthy as those of Ramses II, and must be entirely disregarded in writing the history of this period. The only authentic sources are the accounts of specific campaigns, and on these alone is based the following account of his wars. The early part of this reign seems to have been taken up by cares of state. The land had, it is true, been pacified by Set-necht, but still the reorganization of the state was by no means completed when Ramses came to the throne. In one of his edicts this pharaoh gives orders "To cleanse the temples of Upper Egypt of all that the gods hate, to restore ' the truth ' (i. e., the orthodox faith), and to destroy ' the lie ' (i. e., heterodoxy)." It was owing to this unsettled state of the country that he could not undertake his first campaign, which was an extremely important and absolutely necessary one before his fifth year.

Meanwhile matters looked bad in the Delta. Libyan hordes, under their princes, *Didi*, *Mashaken*, *Tamar*, and *Tjautmar*, had entered the Delta possibly during the period of anarchy which followed on the death of Seti II, and had penetrated to the main stream of the Nile. Here they occupied the banks of the river from *Karbana* to Memphis. In the fifth year of his reign Ramses at last had sufficiently settled the internal affairs of his kingdom to allow of his turning his attention to foreign affairs, and he accordingly marched against the Libyans. After some hard fighting he succeeded in driving them out of the country.

Some three years later the pharaoh was involved in a

more serious war. The "Peoples of the Sea"—the *Shardana, Turusha,* and *Shakarusha,* who in all probability dwelt on the north coast of Africa, and seem to have been great pirates—united with the *Zakkari,. Pursta, Danauna,* and *Ouashouash,* four other seafaring peoples, in a grand raid on the Asiatic coast. They advanced down the coast by land and water, bringing with them their women and children and all their possessions on carts drawn by oxen. All the Syrian people, the *Cheta,* the *Qedi, Karkemish, Aradus,* and *Aresa,* were subdued, and then the mighty stream poured into Palestine, which was mercilessly devastated. Up to this time Ramses had been looking on, an unconcerned spectator, rather rejoiced than otherwise at the downfall of Egypt's old enemies; but as soon as Palestine was invaded, matters assumed a different aspect. Palestine was an Egyptian province, and could not be sacrificed. Accordingly, in the eighth year of his reign, Ramses proceeded against the pirates with a large army and a great fleet. The decisive battle was fought on the coast of Syria, both on land and on sea, and the enemy was utterly routed and almost annihilated. Vast numbers of prisoners were taken. The people concerned in this attack were all seafaring. The *Shardana, Turusha,* and *Shakarusha* we have met before as allies of the Libyan tribes that attacked Egypt in the times of Mer-en-Ptah. They dwelt most probably on the north coast of Africa. That these tribes here appear together with tribes coming most probably from Greece and Asia Minor is no argument against this, for these tribes were bold pirates, ready to join in any enterprise that promised booty. Though we can state with a considerable degree of certainty that the other four tribes came from Greece and Asia Minor, we can not assign to each one its proper home. That Greek tribes took part in this expedition is made extremely probable when we remember that the *Odyssey* mentions raids of this character made by Greek pirates on the Egyptian coast. The threatened invasion was thus happily averted, and the Egyptian domination over Palestine, Phœnicia, and southern Syria considerably strengthened. In these countries the kings of the preceding dynasty had erected and garrisoned forts in order to keep the inhabitants under control. Ramses III went one step further: he tried to force the Egyptian religion—or rather the religion of Amon-Rā—on the Asiatics. A great temple was erected in this region to Amon-Rā, to which, in the language of the official record, "all the peoples of *Chal* (Syria) bring their tribute." Incidentally an expedition against the *Shasu* (Bedouins) of *Seïr* (Edom) is mentioned.

Three years after the great victory over the pirates, the king was again compelled to march against the Libyans. The *Mashawasha*, under their chief *Māshashar*, united with the *Temhu* and *Lebu*, and invaded the western Delta. The pharaoh easily defeated them in a great battle fought on the frontier ; large numbers of the enemy were killed, numerous prisoners were taken, and rich booty was won.

These four wars seem to have been all that Ramses was engaged in. We see that they were all *defensive* wars ; and this is quite a change from the *aggressive* policy pursued by the kings of Dynasties XVIII and XIX. After the close of the second Libyan war, the kingdom was at peace with the world. Aethiopia and Nubia remained tranquil. The trade with Pewent was reopened, a fleet sent there returned laden with the products of its tropical coasts, and brought back with it ambassadors from the various rulers of the region. The copper and malachite mines of the Sinai were operated. The land seemed to have arrived at the highest point of tranquillity and prosperity.

Thus, at least, the official inscriptions and Papyrus Harris I, the official record of this reign, would have us believe. In reality matters were not so pleasant. In the immediate vicinity of the pharaoh's capital, in the necropolis of Thebes, there was almost constant trouble with the laborers. These men were in the government service, and were to receive regular monthly rations ; but the payment was far from regular, and very often they had to strike for them. Thus we know of one gang of laborers that struck for their pay three times inside of half a year, in the twenty-ninth year of this reign. On these occasions they would leave the necropolis in a body with their wives and children, and would not return until their demands had been acceded to. The first strike lasted five days, and, at one stage of the proceedings, matters assumed so serious an aspect that the military had to be called out. The men finally received their dues and returned to work. On the second strike, which occurred a month later, the men marched to the gates of the city, where the governor of Thebes met them, and after some discussion paid them half of their dues, whereupon they returned to the necropolis. Two months later they struck again, but were soon pacified. This record, which no doubt represents the experience of these unfortunates not only during this half a year, but during the entire reign, stands in strange contrast to the accounts given by the official documents.

From another source, too, we learn something more of the real condition of affairs. This is a papyrus giving the minutes of a criminal procedure against several members of the royal family and several high civil and military officers for high treason. Several ladies belonging to the royal harem, headed by Queen *Tey*, who had a son called *Pentaouer*—as the minutes hint, he bore another name, probably he was a son of the king;—formed a conspiracy against the pharaoh. In all probability the conspiracy had for ultimate object the placing of this prince on the throne after his father had been murdered. Most of the harem officials were implicated, the "head over-seer of the harem" even conducting the correspondence for *Tey*. The commander of the troops stationed in Aethiopia, whose sister was in the royal harem, was won over and ordered to revolt against the pharaoh and invade Egypt. Many other officials and army officers were implicated. The conspiracy was, however, betrayed and the conspirators were arrested. A special commission of eleven, vested with extraordinary powers and even permitted to pass sentence of death, was appointed to try this conspiracy case. The commission began its labors, but soon it was found that three of its members had been corrupted, having attended a banquet given them by some of the accused ladies. They were tried, found guilty, and sentenced to have their ears and noses cut off. After this unpleasant interlude, the commission succeeded in accomplishing its labors without further interruption. The conspirators were found guilty and sentenced to death, the nobles being permitted to commit suicide, and the others being executed.

In this reign the power of the priesthood greatly increased. We have already touched on the causes of this,

but there was no pharaoh who did more for the priests‘
and their temples than did Ramses III. The larger part
of the great papyrus Harris I is taken up with lists of
presents given the various temples. The temples of
Amon-Rā, of course, received the lion's share of these
rich gifts, and attained to an unheard-of wealth. Propor-
tionately with the wealth of their temple, the wealth and
influence of the priests· increased. This was the great
mistake of this reign ; but we must say in palliation that
Ramses was but carrying out the policy of his forefathers.

Ramses was a great builder. In all parts of Egypt
we find his name connected with the temples and other
monuments. His chief attention was directed to Thebes
and the Delta. At Thebes he made additions to the
great temple of Amon-Rā, and restored some of the
temples of the necropolis. Following the example of his
great namesake, Ramses II, he built in the necropolis a
temple dedicated to Amon-Rā, and commemorative of his
victories. Behind this temple were the vast treasury-
vaults, in which were stored up the great masses of gold,
silver, precious stones, copper, etc., dedicated to Amon-
Rā, and on the walls are inscribed the records of the immense wealth here deposited. It is probable that these
treasures represent the *state treasury*, placed under the
protection of the god rather than the presents made him.
Before the gates of the temple stood a two-story house,
probably destined to be the residence of the pharaoh and
his attendants on his visits to this city of the dead. At
Tell-el-Yehuda, in the Delta, he built a temple of limestone, alabaster, and granite. Many of the other temples
were repaired by him, and it seems to have required no
small amount of labor to keep the temples of *Qêmet* in
constant repair.

The king died in the thirty-second year of his reign,
shortly after having proclaimed his son Ramses IV co-
regent.

The Successors of Ramses III (1148–1050
B. C.).—The late king had managed to keep Egypt on
much the same level as it had occupied under Ramses II,
but under his successors the prestige of the once all but
almighty ruler of the world rapidly declined. The following pharaohs were all weaklings who could scarcely hold
their own at home, and dared not interfere in foreign af-

fairs. Under them the priesthood that had been greatly favored by Ramses III rose to a commanding position, and the last kings of this line were mere puppets in the hands of the Theban high priests. These rulers cover about a century, but of all this time we have but few monuments of historic value, and two of the most important documents we possess of this time show it in no pleasant light. *Ramses IV, VI, VII,* and *VIII* were brothers; *Ramses V* was a usurper. The very fact that a usurper could ascend the throne after the son of Ramses III shows that there was something wrong somewhere. It is true that we possess a stele on which *Ramses IV* (1148–1137 B. C.) mentions the fact that the Syrians (*Rutenu*) brought tribute; but this is not significant, for southern Syria had been for some time an integral part of the kingdom. Ramses IV sent a great expedition to the Wâdi Hammamât quarries, in the third year of his reign, to quarry stone for temples. He also worked the Sinai copper-mines. Of his buildings but little remains. He seems to have been a "man of promise," but, like most men of his character, he did not keep his promises, and appears as one of the weakest monarchs of his line. He died, or was dethroned, after a reign of only eleven years. *Ramses V* (1136–1132 B. C.), though strong enough to wrest the crown from its legitimate holder, was not able long to retain the position he owed to himself alone; for he reigned but four years. In about 1131 B. C. *Ramses VI,* one of the legitimate heirs of Ramses III, succeeded in ousting the usurper; but he was otherwise of little account—we do not even know how long he reigned. *Ramses VII* and *VIII* were alike unimportant. Of the latter, we know only that he reigned about seven years; of the former, we know nothing. *Ramses IX* holds a rather unenviable prominence among these rulers. Two papyri have come down to us that show how utterly weak and corrupt the government of Egypt was in those days. The first of these contains the minutes of a criminal procedure against a desperate band of robbers that invested the necropolis of Thebes, dated from the nineteenth year of this reign. Some knowledge of the robberies in the necropolis having come to the ears of the governor of Thebes, he immediately, with a view to injuring his enemy, the governor of the necropolis, reported the case to the vizier. This official appointed a commission to investigate the charges. This commission made an investigation, and reported that of *ten* royal pyramids examined only *one* had been entered and robbed, while *all* the private tombs had been broken into and stripped of everything that had any value. During the investigation one of the witnesses, a fellow that bore a desperate character, confessed that he had robbed the tomb of one of the wives of Ramses II, and the investigation proved the truth of his story. Eight robbers were tried and found guilty. Great was the joy of the commissioners, who immediately made public the results of their investigation. The governor of the city, however, whose vague charges had in no way been substantiated, was not satisfied, but openly declared the entire investigation a fraud, and threatened to bring the matter before the pharaoh. After a judicial hearing, the matter was hushed, both sides evidently fearing an official investigation into the conduct of their offices. There was evidently a good deal of crookedness; the governor of the necropolis was undoubtedly guilty at least of criminal negligence, and the commission did their work pretty carelessly, evidently not caring to expose their friend too much.

The second of the above-mentioned papyri is the journal of a gang of laborers employed in the Theban necropolis. We learn from this document that these men were paid in rations of fish, pulse, grain, beer, fat, and fuel; but these provisions were rarely issued on time, and sometimes were not paid at all. In the latter case, the men struck, or, as the Egyptian phrase goes, "lay at home." The journal of this party contains the record of two strikes. The first was peaceable; on the second, they marched to Thebes in a body and laid their complaints before the authorities. Their request for pay was granted, and they returned to work. These strikes give proof of the corruption that was rife in the government. The men's rations were withheld, not because the state could not pay, but because the officials charged with the distribution chose to let the rations disappear. The pharaoh died after a reign of a little more than eighteen years, shortly after proclaiming his son *Ramses X* co-regent. The last three kings of this line are very unimportant. In the early part of the reign of Ramses X, sixty thieves, among them a number of minor government officials and priests of lower grades, were arrested and punished for desecrations and depredations committed in the necropolis. But even the most stringent measures proved of no avail. The great cemetery had grown so enormously that the proper policing of this district was out of the question; and, besides, it would seem that the governor of the necropolis and the chief of its police had a finger in the pie and were not over-vigilant. Ramses X ruled eight years, and was succeeded by *Ramses XI*, of whom we know nothing. *Ramses XII* was the last king of this house. Of him we know little more than that he ruled about twenty-seven years. In his reign there lived a high-priest of Amon and general of the army, *Herīhor*, who became the successor of Ramses. The king was a mere puppet in the hands of the almighty high priest, and it is not to be wondered at that Herīhor finally seized the crown. One of these kings, which one we do not know, was the contemporary of the mighty Assyrian king, *Tiglathpilesar I*, and sent him tribute about 1110 B.C.—a fact that is characteristic of the weakness of these kings.

§ 2. *The Twenty-first Dynasty—The Priest-Kings (1050–950 B. C.).*

We have here again a period that is very obscure. There is some disagreement among historians about the order of succession of the priest-kings; and the fact that Manetho states that the dynasty originated from Tanis has induced some scholars to assume that a Tanitic king had deposed Herīhor, the founder of the dynasty. Such an assumption we consider utterly unwarranted, as it is not consonant with the facts of the case as represented on the monuments. Herīhor and all his descendants were high priests of Amon-Rā in Thebes, and a long line of Herīhor's ancestors occupied the same position. We can trace on the monuments the gradual rise of the high priests of Amon-Rā. We find the high priests *Roī, Amonarnā*, and *Ramsesnecht* mentioned together with the kings on the walls of the temple of Karnak—a distinction enjoyed in the older times only by the co-regent. Under Ramses IX the power of these priests seems to have been still greater; evidently the king was a mere puppet in the hands of Ramsesnecht's son and successor, the high priest *Amenhôtep.* This dignitary no longer inscribed his name with the name of the pharaoh, but declares in the inscriptions that *he* erected this or that building *in the name* of the pharaoh, He rose to the high position of manager of the temple estates, thus holding in his hands all the wealth and influence of the great temples of Amon-Rā.

Sa-Amon Herīhor (1050–1034 B. C.) took the deciding step about 1050 B. C. He had held high offices of trust and honor under Ramses XII, being, to mention only his most exalted offices, high priest of Amon-Rā, chief architect to the pharaoh, general of the army, and head of Upper and Lower Egypt. We see this man thus combined the highest religious, military, and civil offices of the land, and was virtually the ruler. No wonder, then, that on Ramses's death he pushed aside that king's legitimate heir and placed the double crown on his own head. It would seem, however, that Egypt gained but little by the change of rulers. The new king could do no more than preserve the then boundaries of his kingdom; and when we read in his inscriptions that he "repulsed the enemies," we must take this to refer to minor combats with Bedouins, who were constantly prowling about the borders. This pharaoh built chiefly in Karnak, restoring the temple of *Chunsu* (the son of Amon-Rā) and decorating its walls with long religious inscriptions. In one of these inscriptions he had depicted his entire family, consisting of his wife, Queen *Netjemet*, his nineteen sons and grandsons, and five daughters.

The government seems to have remained quite as weak and corrupt as it had been under the last Ramessides, and no wonder, for Herīhor was a descendant of the high pri who so long had governed the land in fact, and he himself had actually ruled the country long before he seized the scepter, so that it was but natural that the old state of affairs continued. Thus the old depredations in the necropolis, instead of ceasing or becoming less, became worse and more desperate than ever. The police of the necropolis were, it is true, not quite efficient, but might have kept the desperadoes in some check had they themselves not been implicated. Accordingly, Herīhor bethought himself of some means of protecting the mummies of his predecessors. The mummies of King Rā-

seqenen, Aahmes I, Amenhôtep I, Thutmosis I, Thutmosis II, Thutmosis III, Ramses I, Seti I, and Ramses II,
were for a while moved about from place to place, and
finally were hid in a shaft at Dêr-el-bahâri, where they
could be better guarded. This shaft was opened in 1881
by Maspero and Brugsch-Bey, and in it were discovered,
besides the mummies already mentioned, those of the
early kings and queens of this dynasty. The mummy of
this pharaoh was not found here, either because it never
was deposited here, or because, like many other objects
found in the shaft, it is still in the hands of the Arabs who
discovered and to some extent plundered this improvised
tomb before the discovery was brought to the attention of
the government. The mummy of Queen Netjemet, cased
in a beautiful sarcophagus of gilt wood, was, however,
found here. Whether or not this king is identical with
a King *Rā-nuter-choper-setep-en-Amon, Meri-Amon-sa-
Amon*, whose name has hitherto been found only in the
Delta, is one of the vexed questions regarding this dynasty. It may be that Herīhor used the title of high-priest
of Amon as coronation-name in Thebes only, while he
adopted another coronation-name for use in Lower Egypt ;
but such a course would seem void of sense. Still, we
have no cause to assume that two kings, one of Upper
and one of Lower Egypt, ruled at the same time. The
whole matter must be laid over until further monuments
are discovered in proof of one or the other hypothesis.
Herīhor ruled about sixteen years.

Herīhor's Successors (1033-945 B. C.).—*Pinetjem I*, the grandson of Herīhor, ascended the throne about
1033 B. C. *Pianchi*, the father of this pharaoh, had been
high priest of Amon-Rā ; but he seems to have died before Herīhor, so that his right to the throne passed to his
son. This king had two wives, Queen *Hathor-hent-taui*
and Queen *Mā-ka-Rā*, of which latter lady an inscription
distinctly says that Amon-Rā had given her the kingdom.
It would seem from this that Mā-ka-Rā was a Ramesside
princess whom Herīhor had compelled to wed his grandson in order to legalize his usurpation—a very common
measure of Egyptian usurpers. At all events, it is a very
curious fact that while the names of both queens are always inclosed in cartouches, that of Pinetjem is without
the cartouche in several inscriptions. Again, there ap-·

pears in a number of inscriptions the name of a King *Cheper-Chā-Rā Pinetjem,* whose wife was Queen *Hathor-hent-taui.* That Pinetjem, the high priest of Amon, and this king are one and the same person there can be no doubt. The mummy of Queen *Mā-ka-Rā* was, like his mummy and that of *Hathor-hent-taui,* found at Dêr-el-behâri. At the feet of *Mā-ka-Rā* was found the mummy of a very young infant designated as "the princess, the wife of the pharaoh, the lady of Both Lands, *Mut-em-hat."* It would seem from this that the infant had been declared the legitimate wife of its father immediately after its birth. This precaution was taken to preclude the chance that any usurper could base claims to the throne on a marriage with this infant. The child and its mother died, however, long before any such eventuality could arise. Pinetjem reigned twenty-five years (1033–1008 B. C.). *Rā-āa-cheper-setep-en-Amon, Pasebchanu I,* the successor of Pinetjem, has left us but few monuments ; but from these we see that like his predecessors he was both high priest of Amon-Rā and King of Egypt. One of his sons named *Pinetjem* was high priest of Amon-Rā under King *Amon-em-apet. Men-cheper-Rā* is another priest-king of whom we know nothing. The same is true of King *Amon-em-apet. Pasebchanu II* has but little significance beyond the fact that his daughter, *Mā-ka-Rā,* became the wife of *Usarken I,* the son of *Shesheng I,* thus legalizing the usurpation of that monarch. Pasebchanu has also some interest for the biblical student. It was in all probability this king who came into connection with King Solomon. He gave Solomon his daughter in marriage, and as a dowry captured for the Jewish king the city of Gaza. There was instituted at this time also a commercial intercourse between Egypt and Israel, the latter state facilitating the trade in horses and wagons between the Egyptians and the Hethites and Aramaens.

§ 3. *The Twenty-second Dynasty.— The Libyan Kings (945–800 B. C.).*

The reader will no doubt remember what was said on a former page concerning the Libyan wars of Seti I and Ramses II, and concerning the ingress of Libyan mercenaries in these reigns. These mercenaries were called *Ma,* an abbreviation of the name of the *Mashawasha* tribe, and their leaders bore the titles of *Ouer-en-Ma*—i. e. "Duke of the Ma," and *Ouer-āa-en-Ma*, "Grand Duke of the Ma." They seemed to have settled in great numbers in the western part of the Delta. The family of one of these leaders, that lived in Bubastis, rose to great power, and finally one of its members, Sheshenq I, succeeded in wresting the scepter from the weak hands of *Pasebchanu II* the last of the priest-kings. The first member of this family who migrated from Libya to Egypt was the *Tehen* (Libyan) *Buiwawa*. He came in about the time of Herīhor. His son *Mausan* already had the title of "Grand Duke of the Ma." In this   his son *Nebnesha* and his grandson *Patut* succeeded him. Patut's son, *Sheshenq*, was married to Princess *Meht-em-oueret*, and their son, *Nemart*, married *Tentespeh*. This latter couple lived about the time of King *Pinetjem*. Their son was Sheshenq I, who on the death of Nemart succeeded him in the offices of Grand Duke of the Ma and commander-in-chief of the army.

Sheshenq I (945–924 B. C.) (the *Shishaq* of the Bible).—An inscription in Abydos shows how highly King Pasebchanu esteemed Sheshenq and his family, for it tells us this monarch kept in repair the tomb of the late Grand Duke Nemart and prayed to Amon-Rā for the success of Sheshenq's arms. Holding the entire power of the land, the army, in his grasp, Sheshenq was the real ruler of Egypt, and it was not at all unnatural that he at length, about 945 B. C., either deposed King Pasebchanu or took advantage of that king's death to become king in name as well as in fact. *Mā-ka-Rā*, the daughter of the late king, was compelled to marry the crown prince *Usarken*, so that he might have a legitimate claim to the throne. That Egypt gained by this change of rulers is an undeniable fact. Immediately after ascending the throne, the new pharaoh issued a stringent edict against all depredations on the property of the dead (the tombs and estates set aside for payment of sacrificial offers were considered the property of the dead) by priests or other persons. This edict proved that he was determined not to tolerate the state of affairs that had existed in the necropolis under his predecessors. The edict in question prescribes the funereal sacrifices for his father. The king expressly states that he had punished those priests that had stolen from the funereal estate. This was no doubt a warning to all inclined to go and do likewise, and seems to have, no doubt backed by an effective police, had the desired effect, for we hear of no further robberies in the Theban necropolis in this and the following reigns.

Early in this reign Jerobōam had fled to his court, He returned to Israel only after the death of Solomon, to become king of the ten tribes. It may be that Sheshenq assisted him to return and gain the throne, as he had married the pharaoh's sister-in-law *Ano*. The most important event of Sheshenq's reign was his Asiatic campaign. He invaded Palestine, and, after overrunning and plundering the country and taking its chief towns, he finally invested and captured the city of Jerusalem in the fifth year of King Rehobōam's reign. The Egyptians sacked the town and carried off, among other things, the treasure Solomon had deposited in the temple. The city is designated as *Yudha Melek*, "the royal Jewish city,"* in the Egyptian inscription treating of this raid.

The king appointed his son *Aauput* high-priest of Amon-Rā, the fattest office in his gift, thus uniting in his family the highest civil, military, and religious powers of the realm. This pharaoh built chiefly in Thebes. At Karnak he began the so-called "Hall of the Bubastides," which was completed by his successors. He died after a reign of about twenty-one years, and Usarken, his son by Queen *Kerāma*, succeeded him.

Sheshenq's Successors.—*Usarken I* (Osarcon) ascended the throne about 923 B. C. He was an unimportant ruler. All we know of him is that he continued the work begun by his father at Karnak, and that his wife, *Mā-ka-Rā*, conveyed all her rights and domains to her family—i. e., her husband and his sons. In consideration of this, her son Sheshenq was proclaimed co-regent and appointed governor of the South, but he never ascended the throne, having in all probability died before Usarken. How long this pharaoh ruled we do not know. On his

* I may mention here that Max Müller, in a recent article, declares that this interpretation of the name is erroneous, and reads *Jad-hamelek*, "Hand of the King," and would find in it the name of a Jewish fort. I do not quite agree with him, and would retain the explanation given in the text.

death, *Takelot I,* son of Queen *Ta-meh-Chunsu,* ascended the throne. Of him we know only that he was married to Queen *Kapes,* and that his son by this lady, *Usarken,* succeeded him. *Usarken II* ruled twenty-three years, and built at Karnak, Bubastis, and other places. The following king, *Takelot II,* was a little more important. In his reign occurred two rebellions, which are, unfortunately, not described in detail. In the eleventh year of his reign a rebellion broke out, where he does not tell us in his inscription, which was subdued. Four years afterward, another text states, "the children of the rebels" attacked Egpyt from the north and from the south, but were repulsed after a long struggle, whereupon they fell into internal dissensions. Unfortunately, these texts do not inform us who these "rebels" and "children of the rebels" were. Possibly we find in these rebellions the beginning of the disintegration of Egypt which was completed at the time the Aethiopian king *Pianchi* invaded the country. Takelot seems to have been strong enough, however, to keep the land together. In the course of the latter text there is a notice that on a certain date the sky had become unrecognizable and the moon had assumed a terrible aspect. After a reign of over fifteen years the king died, and his son *Shesheng III* succeeded him. This pharaoh was the last of this line whose name appears in the inscriptions of Karnak. It would seem that either he or his next successor had been driven out of the capital. He reigned fifty-two years. The last kings of this dynasty— *Pimai, Shesheng IV,* and *Usarken III*—were in all probability confined to the Delta. At the time of *Pianchi's* invasion, Usarken III was King of Bubastis merely, or perhaps divided the Delta with *Aaupet,* King of Clysma.

CHAPTER VIII.

§ 1. *Dynasty XXIII—The Disintegration of Egypt, and the First Aethiopian Invasion.*

ALREADY under Sheshenq III Thebes seems to have been lost to the Libyan dynasty. The last monument that mentions any king of the twenty-second dynasty in Karnak is dated from the twenty-ninth year of Sheshenq's reign ; and after the loss of Thebes these kings were confined to the Delta. Four "kings" are mentioned in the inscription of King *Pianchi,* but we know little of any one of them. They are *Usarken* of *Bubastis,* probably the same man as Usarken III, the last of the Bubastides, *Aaupet* of *Clysma, Nemart* of *Chmunu* (Hermopolis), and *Pefdedbast* of *Chenensuten* (Heracleopolis). Manetho states that Pefdedbast, whom he calls *Petubastis,* reigned forty years. A notice preserved by Ammian, to the effect that in his time the Phœnicians had suddenly attacked and taken Thebes, is probably a faint recollection of the Aethiopian invasion. At all events, the inscription of Pianchi, which mentions besides these four "kings" sixteen rulers of smaller districts, amply proves that Egypt was at this time completely disintegrated.

The Rise of Aethiopia.—We have seen that for many centuries Aethiopia was an Egyptian province, but it would seem that at the close of the twenty-first dynasty it gradually emancipated itself from Egypt. In the times of the twenty-second dynasty Aethiopia was no longer under Egyptian rule. Several historians have attempted to bring into connection the fall of the twenty-first dynasty and the establishment of the Aethiopian kingdom, by assuming that the heirs of Pasebchanu had fled before She-

shenq I to that country early in the tenth century before
the common era, and had founded a theocratic government there. This hypothesis is in some measure confirmed by the name of the first Aethiopian invader of
Egypt, Pianchi, a name that occurs also in the times of
the priest-kings. There is not, however, sufficient proof
to assert this as an established fact. Be that as it may,
we find that, about the time of the twenty-second dynasty,
Aethiopia had become an independent kingdom. The
capital was *Napata*, at the foot of the Gebel Barkal, where
Amenhôtep III had erected a temple to Amon-Rā. The
centuries of dependence had firmly established Egyptian
civilization in Aethiopia. The religion was that of Amon-
Rā, though it was carried out to consequences unknown
in Egypt. The priests had an almost absolute power.
In the name of Amon the kings went out on their wars;
they were entirely dependent on his prophecies and oracles
as interpreted by the priests; they strictly observed the
laws regarding cleanliness and all the minute details of
the ritual. Thus they put into practice what had been
mere theory in Egypt. A long inscription relates how
the king was chosen directly through an oracle of Amon-
Rā, thus confirming the account given by Diodorus. The
priests had, moreover, the right to command the king, in
the name of Amon, to commit suicide, a pernicious practice that *Ergamenes* in the third century B. C. put a stop to.
It is, then, not to be wondered at that the Egyptian priests
described Aethiopia to the Greek tourists as a promised
land. The titulature of the kings was modeled after that
of the pharaohs. The official language of the realm was
the Egyptian, with some dialectic peculiarities; the script
in the older inscriptions is hieroglyphic. Gradually the
language changed more and more, becoming surcharged
with Aethiopian elements, and at last it has changed to
such an extent as to be completely unintelligible. The
script also changed with time; a cursive form known as
the "Meroitic-Demotic script" arose, which no one has yet
succeeded in deciphering. In this script most of the
Aethiopic inscriptions are written, and it is only after this
has been deciphered that we can give a clear picture of
the history of the new Aethiopian kingdom. Early in the
eighth century B. C. the new kingdom was strong enough
to attack Egypt.

II

The disintegration of Egypt offered the then Aethiopian ruler, Pianchi, a fine opportunity of subduing the country that had so long held his native land in subjugation. He invaded Egypt, and seems to have found but little resistance. The inscription which treats of his Egyptian campaign enumerates the twenty sovereigns who at that time ruled Egypt:

1. *Usarken*, King of *Per Bastet* (Bubastis), in the Delta.

2. *Aaupet*, King of *Tenremu* (Clysma), in the Delta.

3. *Nemart*, King of *Chmunu* (Hermopolis magna-Ashumnein), in Upper Egypt.

4. *Pefdedbast*, King of *Chenensuten* (Heracleopolis magna Ahnes), in Upper Egypt.

5. *Tefnacht*, Prince of *Sa* (Sais) and *Mennefer* (Memphis).

6. *Shesheng*, Chief of Mercenaries in *Per-Usiri* (Busiris), in the Delta.

7. *Tjed-Amon-aufānch*, Chief of Mercenaries in *Per-ba-neb-ded* (Mendes), in the Delta.

8. *Anch-Hor*, Chief of Mercenaries in *Per-Thot-up-ro-heh* (Hermopolis).

9. *Bek-en-nef*, Hereditary Prince.

10. *Nesnaketi*, Chief of Mercenaries in the city of *Kaset* (Chois), in the Delta.

11. *Pedubast*, Chief of Mercenaries in *Het-heri-ab* (Athribis), in the Delta.

12. *Patenf*, Chief of Mercenaries in *Per-Sopd*, capital of the twentieth Lower Egyptian nome.

13. *Pama*, Chief of Mercenaries in *Pas-as-rek* (?) (Busiris).

14. *Necht-Hor-nashenu*, Chief of Mercenaries in *Per-Cher-Rer* (?) (*Phagroriopolis*).

15. *Pa-du-Hor-sam-taui*, Priest of Horus in *Sechem* (Setopolis).

16. *Herobusa*, Prince of *Saiut* (Siut) and *Hesaui*.

17. *Tjet-Chiau*, Prince of the City of *Chentnefer*.

18. *Pabas*, Prince of *Cherchau* (Babylon) and *Per-Hāpi* (Nilopolis).

19. A Chief of Mercenaries in *Tanis*.

20. A Chief of Mercenaries in *Ostracine*.

These "kings" and princes seem to have offered but little or no resistance to the Aethiopian invader, and to have remained tranquil under his control for some time. But the spirit of liberty was not dead in the land of Qêmet. In the twenty-first year of Pianchi's reign, an attempt was made by *Tefnacht*, Prince of Sais and Memphis, who was by far the mightiest of these petty sovereigns, to deliver Egypt from the Aethiopian domination. He succeeded in uniting the many petty rulers of Lower and Middle Egypt under his leadership. Then he sailed up the Nile, and everywhere the cities opened their gates to him. At *Chenensuten* he met with the first resistance. King Pefdedbast seemed determined to maintain his separate sovereignty under Pianchi's protection. The city was besieged and taken, but Pefdedbast joined the alliance in only a half-hearted manner. The allies now proceeded south, and at *Chmunu* were joined by King Nemart, who became one of the most useful members of the coalition. They then went against Thebes. Matters were now becoming serious, and Pianchi, on hearing of what was going on, ordered *Pouarma* and *Rā-mer-sekni*, his lord-lieutenants in Upper Egypt to oppose the progress of the rebellion. They immediately took active measures, and began the siege of *Chmunu*. To aid in their operations the Aethiopian king had sent an army north. As they approached Thebes on their fleet, they encountered Tefnacht's fleet. A battle ensued, in which the Egyptians were defeated. Leaving *Rā-mer-sekni* and *Pouarma* to take *Chmunu*, the Aethiopians pursued the fleeing Egyptians northward. The Egyptians made a stand at *Chenensuten*, which city was the key of the Fayoum. Here two battles occurred on succeeding days. The first was fought on the Nile— possibly the Egyptians sought to prevent the enemy from landing—the second was fought on the river-bank at *Perpek*, a town near Chenensuten. In both these battles the patriots were defeated with heavy loss. Meanwhile Chmunu had fallen, and Nemart, hearing of this, determined to retake his capital. Marching rapidly south, he laid siege to the town, and, after defeating several sallies made by the Aethiopian garrison, recaptured it.

Thus matters stood when Pianchi determined to come north and conduct the campaign in person. Before he started, however, his troops had gained some further advantages, taking several smaller fortresses, of which the most important was *Tatehen*. This strong fort was taken

by storm after a most determined resistance ; among the
slain was one of Tefnacht's sons.   Finally, the king came.
After celebrating a religious festival at Thebes he marched
against *Chmunu*.   A regular siege was commenced ; a
high wall was built around the town and a shower of
arrows and stones was thrown into the city.   Three days
the town held out ; but finally Nemart was compelled to
surrender and pay tribute.   Pefdedbast, of Chenensuten,
now came up the stream and paid homage to Pianchi,
bringing him costly presents.   His ready submission proved
that he had joined Tefnacht much against his will, and inclined the king to be gracious.   Pianchi now sailed down-
stream to *Per - Sechem - cheper - Rā* (Illahun), a strong
fortress in the northern part of the Fayoum, which was
surrendered on the first summons.   Just north of this lay
the stronghold of *Meri - Tum* (Meydoum), which seemed
inclined to hold out.   A peremptory summons, leaving
the city the choice between immediate surrender and a
massacre of its garrison in case of a storm, however,
brought the commandant to terms.   At the northern
boundary of Upper Egypt there was a strongly fortified
city which was also surrendered on Pianchi's approach.
This left the way open to Memphis.   The city was very
strongly fortified ; Tefnacht had laid in it a garrison of eight
thousand men, and then gone north, probably to collect
re-enforcements.   The Aethiopian monarch hesitated about
storming the sacred city, and summoned it to surrender,
offering to enter the city peaceably, as his only desire in
coming to Memphis was to pay his homage to the gods.
But Memphis was the key of the Delta, and the garrison
was determined to hold out ; besides, Tefnacht's re-enforcements could be expected daily.   The king, therefore,
ordered his soldiers to storm the town.   They effected a
landing in the harbor of Memphis, and, scaling the walls,
were soon masters of the city.   Many of the garrison
and of the citizens fell in the combat, and many others
were carried off as prisoners of war.   The city was plundered, but the temples were spared, a guard having been
set over them.   Pianchi remained in Memphis several
days, partly to take part in several religious festivals and
partly to receive the tribute of several princes and grand
dukes of the Ma that came here to offer their submission.
He next advanced to *An-Heliopolis*, where he attended

some other religious festivals and received the submission
of a number of other princes, among them *Usarken*, King
of Bubastis. Then he went to *Hat-heri-ab* (Athribis),
where he received the submission of the remaining rebellious princes, except Tefnacht. This leader, deserted
by all his allies, determined to make a last stand for freedom. Razing the walls and burning down the treasury
building of Sais, he retired to the island city of *Mesd* in the
Nile, and strongly intrenched himself. Prince Pefdubast,
of Athribis, was sent against him with a strong detachment. A battle ensued, in which Tefnacht was defeated
and his army annihilated. Tefnacht now sent messengers
to Pianchi, offering to surrender. The king sent him two
ambassadors, in whose presence he swore the oath of
allegiance. Two cities that had hitherto held out now
also surrendered—the rebellion was crushed. After holding a grand reception of the princes, Pianchi returned
home, his ships laden down with the tribute and booty
won in the war.

Pianchi reigned in all forty years, but he had no further
occasion to interfere in Egypt. This was owing to his
wise policy. He left all of the old princes in possession
of their lands, and thus bound them to his person as they
owed their sovereignty to his grace. Moreover, a disunited
Egypt was no menace to him, and the bickerings among
the various petty kings could at any time furnish him a
pretext for invading the country. That he was determined
to prevent the union of these princes was proved by the
great campaign against Tefnacht and his allies. He had
no idea of holding the country, but retired after having
effectually checked Tefnacht's attempt to unite the various
petty states into a great kingdom.

§ 2. *The Twenty fourth Dynasty—Saitic* (B. C. 734-728).

Bekenrenf, the only king of this dynasty, seems to
have succeeded in doing what Tefnacht had attempted
over nineteen years before. According to Diodorus, who
calls him *Bokchoris*, he was the son of *Tnefachthos*, who
is no doubt identical with Tefnacht. For about six years
he ruled undisturbed by the Aethiopians. All we know
of him from the monuments is, that he buried an Apis at
Memphis in the sixth year of his reign.

. In Aethiopia *Kashta* had succeeded Pianchi. This
monarch was married to *Shep-en-apet*, a daughter of
King Usarken, of Bubastis. Their son, *Shabaka*, succeeded him, and immediately determined to conquer
Egypt. He could lay a certain claim to the Egyptian
throne, as his mother was a daughter of the last Bubastide
King. Invading the country, he defeated Bekenrenf—
Manetho states, that he burned him alive—and compelled
the various petty kings to acknowledge his sovereignty.

§ 3. *The Twenty-fifth Dynasty—Aethiopians—The Assyrian Invasions (728-645* B. C.).

Shabaka (the *Sabâkon* of the Greeks, *Sô* of the Bible,
and *Shabé* of the Assyrians, 728-726 B. C.), Herodotus
relates that Sabâkon, the Aethiopian, had conquered
Egypt, and had left it after a reign of fifty years, in consequence of a dream. Diodorus comes nearer the truth
when he states that four Aethiopian kings ruled Egypt for
thirty-six years.

Shabaka took the title of King of Upper and Lower
Egypt, but appointed his sister, *Amenerdas*, who was
married to a man named Pianchi, regent of the country.
The Greek authors praise this ruler highly. He is reputed
to have abolished capital punishment, substituting hard
labor for it. This pharaoh became mixed up in Asiatic
affairs. King Hosea, of Israel, had joined other Syrian
monarchs in a rebellion against Salmanassar IV, King of
Assyria, and the allies had sent to Shabaka, asking his
assistance. The plot was discovered, Hosea was called to
Assyria and thrown into prison. *Salmanassar* invested
Samaria about 725 B. C., but died before the city fell.
His successor, *Sharrukinu* (Sargon) II, continued the
siege, and took the city in 722 B. C. Shortly after a new
coalition was formed, at the head of which stood King
Ilubid, of Hamath. This coalition embraced, besides
Hamath, Arpad, Simyra, Damascus, Gaza, and Egypt.
Sargon was, however, too quick for the allies. Before
Shabaka could join them, Sargon met and routed their
forces at *Karkar*. He now moved southward, and met
Shabaka, who had meanwhile been joined by King
Hanno, of Gaza, at *Raphia*. The allies were badly de-
feated, and Hanno was taken prisoner (720 B. C.). Sar-

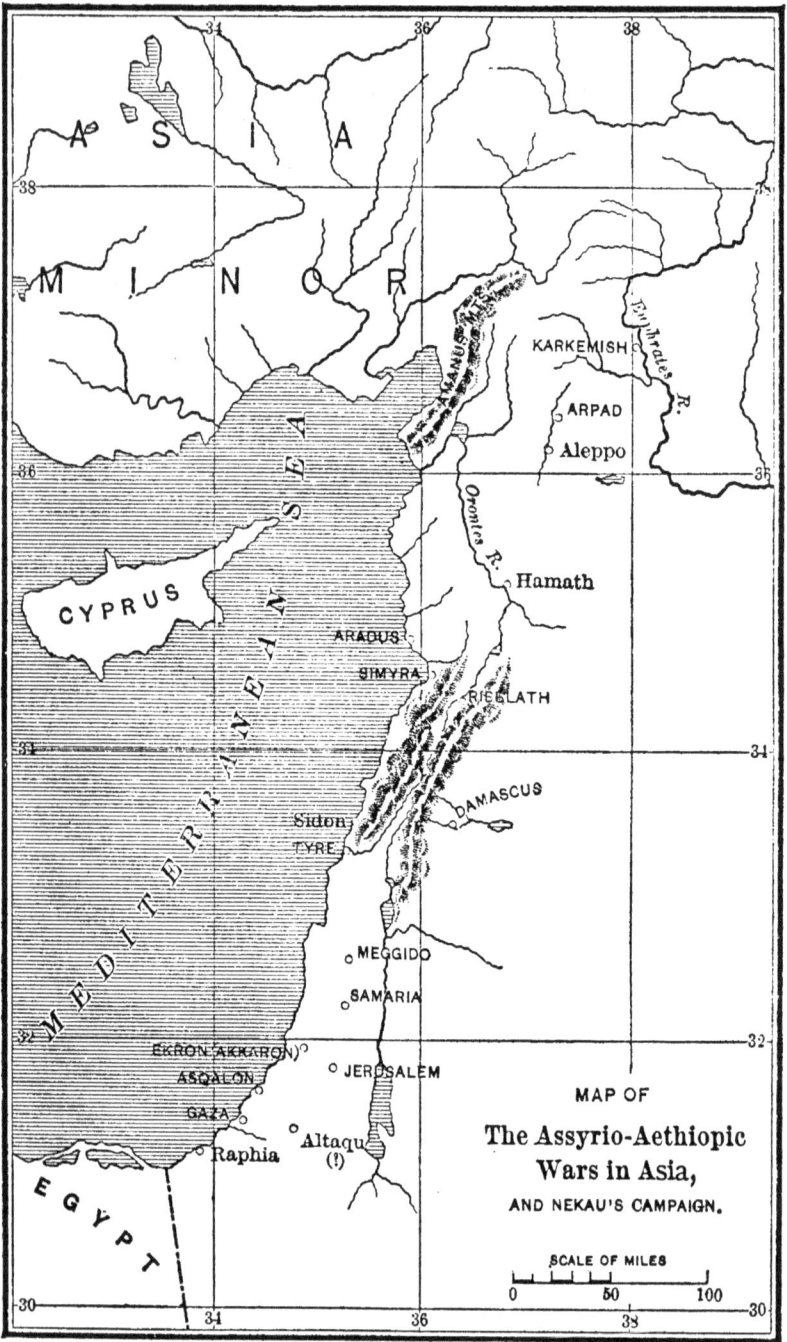

MAP OF

**The Assyrio-Aethiopic
Wars in Asia,**

AND NEKAU'S CAMPAIGN.

SCALE OF MILES

0   50   100

gon could not follow up his victory and invade Egypt, as events had meanwhile occurred in the north which called him to the new seat of war; but he had gained his purpose. *Shabaka* was badly crippled, and even sent tribute. This pharaoh died about 716 B. C.

Shabataka (715–703 B. C.), the successor of Shabaka, is a king of whom we do not know much. Despite the fact that he reigned twelve years, he seems to have done little. In Asia he did not interfere. Probably the defeat of Shabaka at Raphia had been so complete as either to cripple Egypt for years, or at least to discourage her rulers from attacking Assyria again.

Taharqa (702–662 B. C.).—This king was in all probability not of royal parentage, but came to the throne by marrying Shabataka's widow. He was twenty years of age when he ascended the throne. Young and active, he was willing to restore to Egypt its former prestige. Meanwhile Sargon had been assassinated, and his son, *Sin-ahi-erib* (Sanherib), had ascended the Assyrian throne (705 B. C.). Immediately a new coalition was formed against Assyria. Elulaeus of Tyre, Hezekiah of Judah, and Zidkah of Asqalon, formed a league and called upon Taharqa for assistance. *Mardukballadin*, the Chaldean ruler of Babylon, was also drawn into the league and conducted negotiations with Hezekiah. King *Pâdi*, of Akkaron, who had refused to join the rebels, was deposed and turned over to Hezekiah. This mighty coalition if properly handled would have been a match for the Assyrians; but Sanherib was too quick for them. In 701 B. C. he entered Syria and subdued Elulaeus, then going south he took Asqalon and Akkaron. At *Altaqu* he met and defeated Taharqa, who had attempted to check him. After taking Altaqu and some other towns, Sanherib marched on Jerusalem. Hezekiah submitted, and Pâdi was restored to his kingdom. The rebellion was not, however, crushed as yet. Hezekiah continued his negotiations with Taharqa, who had returned to Egypt to collect a new army. Sanherib, hearing of this, accused the Jewish king of treason and threatened him with destruction. Relying on Jehovah and the King of Egypt, Hezekiah boldly held out. Jerusalem was besieged. Meanwhile Taharqa was coming to the aid of his ally with a new army. Sanherib advanced to meet him, but

his army was so reduced by pestilence that he had to retire without giving battle. The story of the Bible is well
known. The angel of the Lord smote the Assyrian army
in the night and one hundred and eighty-five thousand
men died, whereupon Sanherib had to retire. Herodotus
has a somewhat different version of the affair. He relates
that after the Aethiopian Sabâkon, a pious priest of Ptah
named Sethos ruled in Egypt. He denied his soldiers
certain privileges and thus gained their enmity. When
Sanacherib, "king of the Arabians and Assyrians,"
marched against Egypt, they refused to fight, and Sethos
was placed in a sad predicament. He prayed to the gods
for aid, and they sent out mice that ate up the bows and
belts of the Assyrian army encamped about Pelusium
during the night, so that the Egyptian merchants and
mechanics could easily defeat them next day.

The First Assyrian Invasion.—Sanherib never
returned to Palestine. He was assassinated in 681 B. C.,
and his son, *Assarhaddon* (*Ashur-ah-iddin*), ascended
the throne. Trouble between him and Taharqa began in
672 B. C., when King *Ba'al*, of Tyre, relying on promises
of assistance from Taharqa, rebelled against Assyria.
Assarhaddon now determined to put an end to Egyptian
interference. A detachment of his army besieged Tyre,
while the main body marched against Egypt, The prince
of the Bedouins dwelling on the Egyptian border gladly
furnished camels and water, and thus the difficult march
from Raphia to Pelusium was accomplished without serious loss. Taharqa seems to have offered but little resistance, for the Assyrian army entered Memphis, and
soon after Thebes also was taken and sacked. Tabarqa
fled to Aethiopia. After these victories Assarhaddon styled
himself " King of *Musur* (Lower Egypt), *Patrus* (Upper
Egypt), and *Kush* (Aethiopia). The land itself was left
under the control of twenty independent petty sovereigns,
as follows :

1. *Niku-u* (Nekau), of *Mi-im-pi* (Memphis), and *Sa-
ai* (Sais).
2. *Sharru-la-da-ri*, of *Zi-i'nu.*
3. *Pi-sa-an-hu-u*, of *Na-at-hu* (Natho).
4. *Pa-ak-ru-ru*, of *Pi-shap-tu* (*Per-Sopd*, the capital
of the Nomos Arabia, the twentieth Lower Egyptian
nome).

5. *Pu-uk-na-an-ni'-pi* (Bekennef), of *Ha-at-hi-ri-bi* (Hatherïab Athribis).

6. *Na-ah-ki-i*, of *Chi-nen-shi* (Chenensuten).

7. *Pit-tu-bis-ti* (Pedubast), of *Za-a'-nu* (Tanis).

8. *U-na-mu-nu*, of *Na-at-hu*.

9. *Hor-si-ja-i-shu*, of *Tam-mu-u-ti* (Tjeb-nuter Seh-benythos).

10. *Pu-u-a-a-ma* (Pimai), of *Bi-in-di-di* (Per-ba-neb-ded=Mendes).

11. *Su-zi-in-ku* (Sheshenq), of *Pu-si-ri* (Per-Usiri Busiris).

12. *Tap-na-ach-ti* (Tefnacht), of *Pu-nu-bu* (Per-nub).

13. *Pu-uk-ku-na-an-ni-i'-pi*, of *Ah-ni*.

14. *Ip-ti-har-di-i-shu*, of *Pi-sa-at-ti-hu-ru-un-pi*.

15. *Na-ah-ti-hu-ru-an-zi-ni* (Necht-Hor-na - shenu), of *Pi-shab-di-nu-ti*.

16. *Bu-kur-ni-ni-ip*, of *Pa-ah-nu-ti*.

17. *Zi-ha-a*, of *Zi-ja-u-tu* (Siut).

18. *La-mi-in-tu*, of *Hi-mu-ni* (Chmunu).

19. *Ish-pi-ma-a-tu*, of *Ta-a-a-ni* (Teni This).

20. *Ma-an-ti-pi-an-chi* (*Mentu-em-hat*) of *Ni'* (Thebes).

It is impossible for us to identify those of the Assyrian names of Egyptian princes and cities, the Egyptian names of which we have not given. The mightiest of these princes was Nekau (Assyrian *Niku-u*, Greek Necho), Prince of Memphis and Sais (according to Manetho, 671–663 B. C.). He was the favorite of Assarhaddon. At this monarch's request Nekau changed the name of Sais to *Kar-Bêl-Matâti*, "Garden of the Lord of Lands," and gave his son *Psemtek* the Assyrian name *Nabu-ushêzib-an-ni*. Shortly after the conquest of Egypt Assarhaddon resigned the crown in favor of his son *Assurbanipal* (about 668 B. C.).

The Second Assyrian Invasion.—This change in the rulers of Assyria encouraged Taharqa to attempt the delivery of Egypt from Assyrian rule. He advanced on Thebes (Assyr. *Ni'*) and *Mentuemhat* (Assyr. *Manti-pianchi*) received him with open arms, hailing him as a deliverer. Memphis was taken soon after, and the Aethiopian proceeded to make himself at home in Egypt. When Assurbanipal heard of this, he at once determined to punish the Aethiopians. He advanced to *Karbana*, a

town north of Memphis, where he met and utterly routed
Taharqa's forces. The king himself, who had remained
at Memphis, on hearing of this defeat, at once fled to
Thebes, which city he abandoned on the approach of the
Assyrian army without a battle (about 667 B. C.). Meanwhile the Egyptian princes, under the leadership of Nekau
of Sais, Sharladari of Tanis, and Pakruru of Per-Sopd had
opened negotiations with Taharqa, inviting him to renew
his attack, and promising their support. Their letters
were, however, intercepted, and the conspirators were arrested. Proof against them was not wanting, but the Assyrian king evidently thought it wise policy not to punish
them. They were left in possession of their holdings, but
had to swear allegiance to Assurbanipal. Nekau, the
favorite of his father, was sent home loaded down with
presents, and his son Nabu-ushêzib-an-ni was appointed
governor-general of Egypt. Assurbanipal hoped to gain
a powerful ally in this manner, and he was not disap-
pointed.

In the Greek accounts Taharqa figures as a great hero
and conqueror. Strabo relates that he reached the Col-
umns of Hercules (the westernmost point of northern
Africa) on one of his campaigns, and, according to Megos-
thenes, he led his army to India and thence to the Pontus
and Thrace. In his inscriptions he poses as a mighty
conqueror; fourteen negro tribes are mentioned as subdued in Aethiopia. The list of conquered nations he had
inscribed on the walls of the temple of Karnak, is copied
word for word, from that of Ramses II, and even mentions, among other states, Assur, while we know he was
several times whipped by the Assyrians. At Gebel Barkal he built two temples, and at Karnak he repaired portions of the great temple of Amon-Rā and of the temple
of Mut. He died about 664 B. C.

Tanuat-Amon and the Third Assyrian Invasion.—The step-son of Tabarqa ascended the Aethiopian throne about 664 B. C. An inscription found at the
Gebel Barkal relates that this king had been encouraged,
by a dream that promised him the crown of Egypt, to invade that country. Elephantine and Thebes hailed him
as a deliverer; Memphis resisted, but was taken after a
battle. It is very probable that Nekau, Prince of Memphis and Sais, who died about this time (664 B. C.), fell in

one of the battles with Tanuat-Amon. While he was at Memphis a deputation of Egyptian princes, headed by *Pakruru* of *Per-Sopd*, offered their submission. The others withdrew to their fortresses and refused to yield. Tanuat-Amon evidently did not feel strong enough to at- tack them, and preferred to return to Memphis, where he had long theological arguments with those princes who submitted. When Assurbanipal heard of this new Aethi- opian invasion by *Urdamâni* (as the Assyrian inscriptions call Tanuat-Amon), he sent an army against him. The Aethiopians immediately withdrew before the approach of the Assyrians, and fled to Aethiopia. Thus, about 662 B. C., was driven from Egypt the last Aethiopian king who dared invade the country.

12

CHAPTER IX.

THE EGYPTIAN RENAISSANCE—DYNASTY XXVI (645–525 B. C.).

§ 1. *Psemtek I (645–610* B. C.).

WE have seen in the preceding chapter how the house of Sais gradually rose in importance. The first *ati*—as the Egyptians called the petty sovereigns of the preceding epoch—of this line that succeeded in gaining supreme power, even though for a short time only, was *Tefnacht*, the contemporary of Usarken III, King of Bubastis, and the great opponent of Pianchi. How his attempt at unifying Egypt failed we have already seen. A descendant of his was the *Bekenrenf*, who ruled at least in Lower Egypt for six years (734–728 B. C.). The next prince we know is *Nekau*, the favorite of Assarhaddon and Assurbanipal. As predecessors of this Nekau, Manetho mentions *Stephanites* (ruled seven years) and *Nechepsos* (ruled six years), the Egyptian names of which princes are unknown. This Nekau seems to have come to his death about the time Tanuat-Amon invaded Egypt (664 B. C.). Nekau was succeeded by his son Psemtek, the Psametichos of the Greeks, who was given the name of *Nabu-ushêzib-anni* at Assurbanipal's request. Psemtek seems to have been a faithful ally of Assyria for quite some while, but he merely waited a chance to gain his independence. He entered into friendly relations with Tanuat-Amon, marrying one of his relatives—the Aethiopian princess *Shep-en-apet*, a daughter of Queen *Amonerdas*. As Amonerdas had been Queen of Egypt, Psemtek thus acquired a claim to the throne. At length the right moment came, about 645 B. C. Aided by mercenaries sent him by King Gyges, of Lydia, he succeeded in making himself independent from Assyria. It is evident that he succeeded in this only after a struggle, but we have no record of his combats with Assyria. His next enemies were in Egypt itself. Though he was un-doubtedly the rightful ·sovereign of the country, yet the many petty rulers that divided the country among them-selves did not submit without a struggle. Psemtek, how-ever, succeeded in gaining the ascendency and uniting Egypt under his scepter. Psemtek made *Sais* his capital. This made *Neit*, the great goddess of Sais, the official head of the national pantheon, and deposed Amon-Rā, who had held this position, with some interruptions, for about fifteen hundred years. Memphis, the oldest capital of Egypt, and part of Psemtek's original principality, was also highly favored, and many of the government offices were located there. Thebes was falling into decay; the Assyrian wars had dealt the city a blow from which it never recovered. True, Psemtek and some of his suc-cessors built here and repaired the great temple of Amon, but the city never again rose into prominence. Of the city of Sais there remains to-day scarce a trace; the cli-mate and soil of the Delta are not favorable to the pres-ervation of ruins, and after the city had once fallen into decay all traces of it rapidly disappeared.

Mindful of the great debt he owed the Greek merce-naries, Psemtek little by little increased them. By this action he incensed the native mercenaries, who had bith-erto ruled supreme in Egypt. According to Herodotus, two hundred and forty thousand men of the warriors "who stood on the left of the king" emigrated to Aethiopia in this reign because they had not been relieved in their gar-risons for three years. This story is assuredly untrue, but it reflects the fact that the native troops were highly dis-satisfied, and were no particular friends of Psemtek's.

The stories that the Greek authors tell us of his scien-tific experiments to ascertain which people was the oldest of the world, and those that they relate of his efforts to find the source of the Nile, are all alike untrue and legend-ary. The remark of Strabo that he was one of the great-est conquerors of the world is also false. The king was too much occupied with internal affairs to go in search of foreign conquest. The real fact of the matter is, that Psemtek was confined to Egypt proper. On the western frontier he fortified Marea as a defense· against Libya; on the Asiatic frontier he erected the strong fortress of

Daphnæ near Pelusium, and on the Aethiopic frontier the town of *Souen* (Assuan, Syene) was strongly fortified. The fact that the three frontiers were thus put in a state of defense proves that the king did not make any conquests. Herodotus relates that he conquered Asdôd after a siege of twenty-nine years, but there is no reason to believe this.

The policy of this king and of all his successors was to gain the friendship of the Greeks. He gave lands along the banks of the Pelusian branch of the Nile, near Bubastis, to the Ionians and Carians, and, in order that they might come into communication with his subjects, he gave them Egyptian boys whom they should teach Greek and who were to serve as interpreters. The Milesians soon after entered the Bolbitic arm of the Nile and settled a fortified camp, which was called the Milesian camp. Tyrian merchants settled possibly about the same time in Memphis, and gave their name to the Tyrian quarter of this city. The king died about 610 B. C., having been Prince of Sais and Memphis from 664 B. C., and king from 645 B..C. on.

§ 2. *Nekau* (*Greek Necho and Nechâo*)—(*610-594* B. C.).

Nekau successfully continued the policy of his father. Herodotus relates that he began the construction of a canal which was to connect the Nile with the Red Sea, and that, after a hundred and twenty thousand laborers had perished, Nekau suddenly stopped the work, having been warned by an oracle that he was working for the barbarians. This story is very improbable. A canal connecting the Nile with the Red Sea existed already in the times of Seti I and Ramses II, about seven hundred years before this time. This canal was mentioned in the Assyrian inscriptions of the eighth century B. C., and it is scarcely possible that it could have disappeared entirely in less than a century. Nekau possibly cleared it of sand and widened it. The story of the enormous number of laborers who perished during the progress of the work and that of the oracle are both utterly false.

Herodotus relates a story of a great maritime enterprise undertaken at this time which seems quite credible. He states that Nekau sent out Phœnician ships from the

Red Sea to circumnavigate Africa, and that in the third year of their journey they returned to the Mediterranean through the Straits of Gibraltar. The very fact that Herodotus questions—namely, that in circumnavigating "Libya" (i. e., Africa) they had the sun on their right hand—proves that they really did accomplish their task. The same historian relates that Nekau kept fleets of triremes in the Mediterranean and the Red Sea.

Nekau felt himself strong enough to attempt the restoration of Egyptian supremacy in Asia. Great changes had meanwhile taken place on this continent. *Assurbanipal* died the king of a great empire, but his successors were not able to hold their own. About 608 B. C., *Nabopallassar*, whom *Assurbanipal* had appointed Viceroy of Babylon, threw off the Assyrian yoke and founded an independent Babylonian kingdom. Intent on crushing out the Assyrian kingdom, he allied himself with King *Kyaxares*, of Media, and together they attacked and completely annihilated the Assyrian kingdom. The Medes kept all the land east and north of the Tigris, the Babylonians Mesopotamia and Syria. Nekau thought the time had now come to intervene in Asia. Accordingly, in the spring of the year 608 B. C., he invaded the continent. He encountered no resistance until he reached Megiddo. Here, at the very spot where, almost a thousand years before, Thutmosis III had defeated the Syrian coalition, King Josia, of Judah, had drawn up his army ready to dispute Nekau's advance. The pharaoh, not wishing to lose time in subduing the petty sovereigns of Syria and Palestine, haughtily ordered the Jewish king to give way. Josia refused, and was arranging his army for the coming battle, when he was fatally wounded by an arrow. The king was brought back to Jerusalem, where he died and was buried amid the wailings of his people, over whom he had ruled for thirty-nine years. Nekau continued his march to Ribla, near Hamath, where he went into camp. Meanwhile the Jews had elected Joachas, the son of Josia, king, but Nekau was dissatisfied with their choice and deposed him, giving the kingdom to his older brother Jojaqîm, and levying a heavy contribution on the land. Excepting Judea, Gaza was the only state that offered any resistance to the Egyptians. Up to the year 604 B. C. Nekau seems to have had his own way in Asia, but in that year Nabopallassar was ready to meet him.   He himself was old and sick ; so he sent his son *Nebuchadnez-zar* (Bab., *Nabu-kudurri-uzzur*) against the Egyptians. At Karkemish, on the banks of the Euphrates, the two armies met, and Nekan was utterly routed.   His army must have been completely annihilated, for he left Syria to the victor, without daring to oppose him again.   Nebu-chadnezzar probably had the intention of invading Egypt, but the death of his father compelled him to return to Babylon.   Nekau did not dare to interfere in Asia again. Time and again the Jews begged him for assistance in their repeated revolts against the Babylonians.   At last Jerusalem fell, about 596 B. C., and Nebuchadnezzar was free to invade Egypt ; but it seems that he was called to other parts of his kingdom, and the threatened invasion did not come until much later.   Nekau died in 594 B. C., and was buried, like his father, in Sais.

§ 3. *Psemtek II (594–589 B. C.).*

The only historical event of this short reign was an invasion of Aethiopia.   Both Herodotus and Aristeas mention it, and an Egyptian inscription confirms their report.   Late in this reign General *Nes-Hor* was sent against the Aethiopians, and the war was finally brought to a close early in the following reign.   It may be that the trouble with Aethiopia had begun already in Nekau's time, and this would account for his otherwise incom-prehensible policy with regard to the Jewish rebellions. The *grafiti* left on the colossi of Abu-Simbel by the Phœ-nician and Greek mercenaries that marched with the Egyptian army on this campaign, still further confirm the report of Psemtek's war in this quarter.   Despite his short reign of only six years, this pharaoh was an active builder, restoring and repairing temples in all parts of Egypt, from the Delta to Nubia.

§ 4. *Ouahabrā (Greek Apries, 589–564 B. C.).*

Early in this reign *Nes-Hor* brought to a successful conclusion the Aethiopian war begun in the reign of Psemtek II.   Ouahabrā thought matters in Asia favored an intervention on his part.   In Judea important changes had taken place in the times of his predecessors. Jojaqîm, the king whom Nekau had appointed, was deposed in 597 B. C., after a reign of eleven years, and Jojachim, his son, put in his place by Nebuchadnezzar. Soon after he also was deposed, and Zedekiah put in his place. Zedekiah (596–586 B. C.) was not the man the Babylonian king had thought him. He determined, despite the warnings of the prophets, to win the independence of his kingdom. Ouahabrā now came to his aid and began a war with Tyre. Sidon was taken, and a Cypriote fleet that opposed him was utterly defeated. Although thus far successful, the pharaoh withdrew soon after, on the approach of the Babylonians. Meanwhile Zedekiah had begun the war, but Jerusalem was soon invested, and, after a spirited resistance, was taken (July, 587 B. C.), while Ouahabrā did nothing to assist his sorely beset ally. Zedekiah was deposed and blinded, and Gedalia was set on the throne. He was assassinated by a descendant of the family of Ishmael, who was soon after compelled to fly the country. He and his friends went to Egypt, where Ouahabrā received them kindly.

Soon after Ouahabrā began a war which promised better results. A war had broken out between the Greek city of Cyrene, which lay on the northern coast of Africa, west of Egypt, and the Libyans. The Libyan king *Adikram* placed himself under the protectorate of Egypt, and an Egyptian army was immediately sent out to aid him. At the town of Irsa, on the well of Thestis, a battle ensued, in which the Egyptian army was annihilated. This account, taken from Herodotus, is probably correct, but the rest of his account is certainly false. He relates that the Egyptians were furious over the defeat, and declared that Apries had sent out the native troops in order to have them annihilated, so that his rule over the rest of the Egyptians might be the more secure. This is entirely unnatural. In Egypt the pharaoh was an absolute ruler; he was considered as the son of the god Rā and the incarnation of the god Horus, and it would not have been at all necessary for him to destroy the national troops in order to strengthen his rule. The troops, according to Herodotus, also murmured, and the king sent an officer named Amasis (Egyptian, *Aahmes*) to quiet them. While he was addressing them, a soldier, stepping behind him, placed a helmet on his head and proclaimed him king. The rest of the army shouted their assent, and Amasis, gladly accepting the election, placed himself at their head and marched against the pharaoh. A messenger sent by Apries was sent back with a sarcastic reply. Apries now prepared for battle, and, collecting his Greek mercenaries to the number of thirty thousand, marched against his rival. At Momemphis, on the Canopic branch of the Nile, the armies met, and Apries was, after a well-contested battle, defeated, captured, and brought to Memphis, where he was kept in prison for a while, but was finally delivered up to the angry populace and strangled. This story is utterly false from beginning to end, as are also the many anecdotes the Greek writers tell of Amasis.

We know, however, that Ouahabrā, about six years before his death, appointed Aahmes II co-regent. Aahmes was wedded to *Anchnes-nefer-ab-Rā*, a daughter of Pscmtek II, and to *Neit-aqert*, a sister of Ouahabrā. These facts completely refute the Greek legends. Why Aahmes was appointed co-regent we can not say; possibly the king had no male issue, and wished to keep the succession in the family.

In the time of their joint reign fell Nebuchadnezzar's invasion. This campaign was undertaken, according to the Babylonian inscriptions, in the thirty-seventh year of Nebuchadnezzar's reign—i. e., in 567 B. C. The Babylonians found little or no resistance, and easily succeeded in overrunning and plundering the whole land as far as Assuan, and then retired either voluntarily or after having been defeated by Nes-Hor. Be that as it may, the Babylonians never again entered Egypt. Ouahabrā died in 564 B. C., after having ruled twenty-five years in all, nineteen alone and six in conjunction with his brother-in-law and successor.

§ 5. Aahmes II (Amasis, 564–526 B. C.).

This pharaoh came into still closer connection with the Greeks than any of his predecessors. The many anecdotes the Greek authors tell of his private life and family relations are all untrustworthy, as are also the reports that Pythagoras, Solon, and Thales visited Egypt in his reign. Solon is even said to have copied from Amasis' laws one of the laws he promulgated at Athens in 594 B. C., a statement that is of course absurd. Further, this king is said to have entered into friendly relations with Cleobulus, Bias, and Pittacus, and to have foreseen the downfall of Polycrates. All of these stories, which are, by the by, chronologically impossible, have a direct tendency, namely, to prove that all of the knowledge and philosophy of Greece was derived from Egypt. Amasis being the king best known to the Greeks, they placed the Egyptian voyages of their sages in his reign. We have already alluded to these traditions in the introduction.

More credible are the accounts the Greek writers give us of his wars. He fought against the Arabians (i. e., the Asiatics), and, in order to increase the valor of his troops, he had the statues of the chief divinities set up behind their ranks, so that the troops believed the gods themselves were observing them. He next sent out a fleet against Cyprus that succeeded in subduing the Cypriote cities, which remained Egyptian dependencies for some time thereafter. This expedition was most probably undertaken as part of Egypt's work in the great coalition which had been formed for the purpose of checking, if possible, the rise of the new Persian monarchy. This coalition was joined by Egypt, Lydia, Babylon, and Sparta. The object was to attack Persia from three sides at once, and, had the allies acted in concert, and not wasted valuable time over their preparations, they might have crushed Cyrus. As it was, Crœsus moved before the others were ready, and all the help he could get from his allies consisted in a detachment of troops sent him by Aahmes. In the spring of 546 B. C. he entered Cappadocia, devastated the country, and captured the strong fortress of Pteria. Now was the time for Aahmes and Nabunaid, King of Babylon, to act; but it was impossible for them to concentrate their forces and to co-operate properly. Cyrus first moved against Crœsus, and soon had conquered Lydia, taken its capital, and made the king a prisoner (fall of 546 B. C.). A Persian fleet sent against Cyprus easily succeeded in dislodging the Egyptian garrisons. Aahmes now, instead of coming to the aid of his ally, Nabunaid, remained inactive while the Persians conquered Babylon and took possession of Palestine and Syria as far as the Egyptian frontier. The pharaoh evidently hoped to pacify Cyrus by this inactivity; but he had gone just one step too far, and had incurred the determined enmity of the Persians. That the invasion of Egypt did not follow immediately on the occupation of Palestine was owing to complications that had arisen on the eastern frontier. In the wars fought here Cyrus lost his life; but his successor, Cambyses, soon punished Egypt for its share in the coalition against Persia.

Aahmes thought it to his advantage to interfere in Cyrenæ. Here King Arkesilaus had been assassinated by Learchus, who had ascended the throne, and, supported by Egyptian mercenaries, had instituted a most tyrannical rule. His misrule did not last long. He was assassinated at the instigation of Polyarchus and his sister Eryxo, who placed Battus, the son of Arkesilaus, on the throne. The Egyptian mercenaries now called on Aahmes for aid, and he determined to take advantage of these conditions to subdue the city. Before he started on the expedition, however, his mother died, and he was detained in Egypt by the preparations for her interment. Polyarchus, accompanied by his mother Critola and his sister Eryxo, now went to Egypt to propitiate the pharaoh. Aahmes received them kindly, and praising the energy they had shown, dismissed them, loaded with presents. He now abandoned the expedition against Cyrenæ, as he was evidently satisfied with the recognition of his sovereignty. The two nations hereafter remained at peace until the downfall of Egypt.

Aahmes was confined entirely to Egypt. His expedition against Cyprus, though at first successful, had proved in the end a failure; in Asia he dared not interfere; Aethiopia retained its independence, and his sovereignty over Cyrenæ was purely nominal. While the kingdom thus did not extend its boundaries under Aahmes, still his reign was an epoch of great prosperity. Agriculture and commerce flourished, and it is stated that there were at this time twenty thousand inhabited places in Egypt.

The Greeks were, of course, greatly favored; and costly presents were made to their temples, among them being a contribution of a thousand pounds of alum, one of the most important raw products of Egypt, to the fund the Amphictyons were collecting for rebuilding the Delphic temple. Greek immigration was greatly encouraged. The Ionians and Carians, whom Psemtek I had settled on the Pelusic branch of the Nile, were removed to Memphis to serve as a body-guard to the pharaoh. In place of the harbor thus lost to the Greeks, the king gave them the city of Naucratis and its surroundings, in the neighborhood of the present city of Alexandria. This new city stood outside of the pale of Egyptian jurisdiction, and was allowed to make its own laws. The result was, that the inhabitants clung to their own Greek customs and institutions with the greatest tenacity, and went their way entirely uninfluenced by their Egyptian neighbors. The city being originally intended for Ionians from Teos, its government was modeled after that of the latter city. This town became the center of Greek activity in Egypt. In it was erected the great sanctuary of the Greeks in Egypt; this was the Helleneion, which was built by several Greek cities conjointly. These cities were Chios, Teos, Phocæa, Clazomenæ, Cnidos, Halicarnassus, Phaselis, and Mytilene. The reason why so many cities helped to build the Helleneion was, that all of the cities that took part in this work had the privilege of sending to Naucratis a "supervisor of trade," or, as we would put it, appointing a member of the board of trade. Temples to Zeus, Hera, and Apollo were also built by other cities, who thus gained the same privilege as the builders of the Helleneion. Naucratis rose very rapidly, owing to certain laws that gave her a complete monopoly of the trade with Greece. The Greeks soon had colonies in all parts of Egypt, even in the southern portions of the country. The Milesians had a trading post at Abydos, and Samian merchants even settled in the Great Oasis.

Being engaged in no great wars, this pharaoh was enabled to devote considerable attention to the temples of the land. In all parts of Egypt, from the Delta to the island of Bigeh, we find traces of his work. He died 526 B. C., after having been co-regent of his brother-in-law for six years and sole ruler for thirty-eight years.

§ 6. *Psemtek III and the Persian Conquest of Egypt*
(*526-525* B. C.).

When Psemtek III ascended the throne of his fathers, the catastrophe that had so long threatened the land at length overwhelmed it. The account of this catastrophe has been preserved to us by Herodotus. The stories that, according to Greek traditions, impelled Cambyses to invade Egypt are all untrustworthy, as they seek to bring Cambyses into relationship with the Egyptian kings and to find the cause of the war in this relationship, while making Cambyses appear, at the same time, as the legitimate pharaoh. The war, far from having any such cause as the Greek historians would have us believe, had, in all probability, been determined on already by Cyrus, who was prevented from carrying out this part of his plan by other matters. Cambyses was free to attack Egypt, and he had ample cause for war in the fact that Egypt had been the ally of his father's worst enemies, King Crœsus of Lydia and King Nabunaid of Babylon.

Accordingly, Cambyses began making active preparations for the war, and everything indicated that he was going to have a hard time of it. The eastern frontier of Egypt was protected by the Syrian Desert that skirted it, to cross which was a task of no small difficulty. Recognizing this fact, Aahmes had concentrated his forces at Pelusium, hoping to gain an easy victory over the Persian army, which no doubt would suffer terribly in the desert, and reach the Egyptian border sadly used up. Cambyses did not underrate the difficulty of the undertaking, and made the most extensive preparations. A great fleet was fitted out to attack Pelusium by sea, while the army attacked it by land. Just as he was about to start, he received unexpected and timely aid, In the Egyptian army there was a Halicarnassian officer named Phanes, a bright and able leader who had had some difficulty with Aahmes. In consequence of this he had fled to the Persian monarch. On the way he was overtaken by the king's favorite eunuch, but managed to escape. Shortly after this event Aahmes had died, and Psemtek III had succeeded him. Phanes not only betrayed to the Persians all the secrets of the state, but he also showed them the means of crossing the desert without great loss. To accomplish this, envoys

were sent to all the Bedouin sheiks of the desert, and treaties were concluded with them. They agreed to furnish
the army with camels and water, and thus the Persian
army was enabled to cross the desert and to reach Pelusium with but little loss. The battle that ensued was
waged with great fury; but, finally, after both sides had
lost heavily, the Persians were victorious, and the Egyptians fled from the field. Pelusium surrendered soon after.
A ship was now sent to Memphis, whither the pharaoh
had fled, to demand the city's surrender. When it entered the harbor of Memphis the garrison boarded it,
killed the crew, and destroyed the vessel. This breach
of international usage met with a severe but well-merited
punishment. Memphis was besieged and taken. Ten
days after the capture the punishment came : two thousand
sons of the most respected citizens, among them the son
of King Psemtek, were executed, to atone for the death of
the two hundred men that had composed the crew of the
ill-fated vessel. The daughter of the pharaoh and the
noblest virgins were sold into slavery, and the fortunes of
the richest citizens and of the king's friends were confis-
cated, leaving their former owners beggars. The fate of
Psemtek was comparatively light, Cambyses even intending
to make him governor of Egypt, but he became involved
in a conspiracy against Cambyses, and was compelled to
take poison. Thus ended the last of the Psemteks.

As a result of the capture of Memphis, the Libyans
submitted voluntarily, and paid tribute. Cyrenæ and Barcæa also sent tribute, but this the Persian monarch divided among his soldiers, as he hoped to gain far more by
capturing these rich towns than he could ever get from
them as voluntary tribute.

13

CHAPTER X.

§ 1. *The Twenty-seventh Dynasty—Persians (525–414 B. C.).*

Cambyses (525–522 B. C.).—The fall of Memphis seems to have sealed the fate of Egypt. The rest of the country in all probability submitted peaceably; the very fact that the Libyans, Barcæa, and Cyrenæ offered their submission and sent tribute right after the capture of Memphis proves that from that time on the Persian monarch was the undisputed ruler of Egypt. Cambyses appointed Aryandes satrap of Egypt, but seems not to have changed any of the laws and institutions of the land.

Shortly after Memphis surrendered, the king paid a visit to Sais, the then capital of Egypt. The stories that Herodotus relates of outrages committed here by Cambyses are unhistorical, being utterly disproved by an inscription on the statue of the hereditary prince, *Hor-utja-suten-net*, who had been keeper of the seal, chief scribe of the palace, admiral of the fleet, chief physician, etc., under Aahmes II and Psemtek III. This man relates that *Kembut* (Cambyses) came to Egypt and ruled all the land, remaining as King of Egypt, and taking the coronation name of *Mesut-Rā*. Hor-utja-suten-net was appointed by him chief physician and superintendent of the palace. He initiated the king into the mysteries of the goddess Neit, and described to him her temple. He now complained of the Persian soldiery that had taken quarters in the temple, and begged that they be removed so that the temple might be clean again. The king ordered that the temple be cleansed, that all of her servants be restored to the goddess, and that her festivals be celebrated as of yore. When the king came to Sais he went to the temple of Neit, worshiped her, and sacrificed to her and all the other gods of Sais ; in short, conducted all the sacred cere- monies the same as every former king had done. He also ordered Hor-utja-suten-net to prepare an inventory of all the temple utensils, and to erect buildings for the goddess. We see that the Persian monarch strove to ap- pear as the successor of the pharaohs—a policy he pursued until his understanding was clouded by insanity.

Cambyses now determined to conquer the rest of Africa. Three expeditions were planned—one against Carthage, another against the Oasis of Amon, and a third against Aethiopia. The first of these expeditions was never undertaken, as the Phœnicians, who made up the greater part of the Persian fleet, refused to serve against Carthage ; and Cambyses, owing to the fact that they had joined him voluntarily, did not dare to force them. The expedition against the Oasis of Amon proved a failure. An army of fifty thousand men started from Thebes and marched through the Sahara to the Greek town of Oasis. After they left this smaller oasis no news of them ever reached Egypt ; in all probability they perished in a sand- storm. The expedition against Aethiopia was in the main successful, although the Greek historians strove to give the impression that it was a failure. Besides the half- legendary account of Herodotus, according to which pro- visions gave out on the march, and the men after eating their beasts of burden were compelled to resort to canni- balism, we have no full account of this campaign. But the fact that Aethiopian troops fought against the Greeks under Xerxes, and the mention by Ptolemy and Pliny of a town, *Cambyson Tamieia*, in Aethiopia, prove that the campaign was successful. Moreover, Strabo and others relate that Cambyses captured the capital of Aethiopia, and named it *Meroë*, after his sister. As the army was returning, a sand-storm overtook it near the First Cataract, and the greater part of the one hundred and fifty thousand men perished. Only a fragment of the great army re- turned to Egypt. Cambyses had, however, fully accom- plished his object : he had thoroughly subdued Egypt, and secured it against foreign invasion.

On his return from Aethiopia a great change came

over the spirit of his reign. From early youth he had
been subject to epileptic fits, and now he became insane.
His insanity seems to have first broken out in Memphis,
at the festival of the enthroning of an Apis-steer. While
the king was warring in Aethiopia the old Apis-steer had
died, and shortly before his return a new one had been
found. As he entered Memphis he found, according to
Herodotus, the citizens celebrating a great festival. This
naturally angered him, as he supposed they were rejoicing
over the loss of his army. So he summoned the elders of
the city before him and asked them why the Egyptians
were celebrating a festival, now that he was returning after
meeting with so severe a loss, and had celebrated no festival when he first came. They replied that a god had
been born to the Egyptians, whose birth was always celebrated in this manner; and the king had them executed
as liars. He then sent for the priests, and, on questioning
them, received the same answer. Now he made further
inquiries regarding the god, and finally ordered the sacred
steer to be brought before him. When the animal was
brought, the king drew his sword, intending to kill it, but
succeeded only in wounding it on the thigh. Then he
scoffed at the priests, telling them their god was only flesh
and blood, after all. He now had the priests scourged,
and had all persons who took part in the festival killed.
The Apis died of his wound soon afterward, and was se-
cretly interred by the priests. While this account is certainly overdrawn, we have no reason to doubt that the
killing of the Apis is historical, for this does not seem to
have been the only sacrilege the king was guilty of. He
is accused of having made fun of the statues of Ptah,
which represent the god as a dwarf, and of having robbed
temples and burned several statues of gods. These outrages were no doubt all committed after he had become
insane, for the inscription of Hor-utja-suten-net proves
that in the early part of his reign this king had everywhere
sought to imitate the pharaohs. The Greek historians
were naturally prejudiced against him, and strove to make
him appear as a wild, remorseless tyrant, in glaring contrast to his father Cyrus, whom they depicted as an ideal
ruler. The whole history of Cambyses was written by Herodotus from an unhistorical standpoint. His object was
to make this reign a grand tragedy: the king was a wild,

insane tyrant, and his violent death was a punishment for his many sins against the gods and men. This may be *tragedy*, but it certainly is not *history*.

Persia itself suffered from the insanity of the king just as much as did Egypt. Cambyses's greatest crime was the murder of his brother *Bardja*, whom he had assassinated by *Prexaspes*. He is also accused of having attempted to murder Crœsus, the old friend of his father, and of having killed the son of Prexaspes while drunk. At last the end came. Cambyses had for unknown reasons gone to Syria. Here news of a revolt in Persia reached him. He had before leaving Persia appointed *Patizeithes*, a Magian, superintendent of the palace. This man knew of the murder of Bardja, and determined to make use of his knowledge. He had a brother named *Gaumata*, who closely resembled the murdered prince. This brother he placed on the throne, and proclaimed through all the land that Bardja had ascended the throne of Persia. Cambyses easily convinced himself that this so-called Bardja was a swindler, and determined to suppress the revolt. As he was about to start out on this expedition, he accidentally wounded himself—tradition asserts in the thigh, the same place where he wounded the Apis—and of this wound he died. Before his death, however, he assembled his nobles about his bed, confessed the murder of Bardja, and urged them to punish the Median usurper.

Darius I (Eg., *Antliush*, 521-485 B. C.).—For a while the Persian nobles remained inactive, fearing to divulge the murder of Bardja; but finally, in 521 B. C., *Darius*, the son of *Hystaspes*, who was the next heir to the throne, Cambyses having died childless, with six companions succeeded in slaying the usurper. As Hystaspes declined the crown, Darius now became King of Persia. The new king was compelled to combat with several usurpers in Persia, but Egypt remained loyal. Aryandes, the satrap appointed by Cambyses, had been left in office by Darius. He felt sufficiently strong to attempt the extension of the Persian power in Africa. A fine opportunity to do this soon offered itself. When Cambyses invaded Egypt, Cyrenæ had voluntarily submitted and paid tribute. King Arkesilaus III made about this time a trip to Barcæa, after having appointed his mother, Pheretime, regent. Here he was murdered by some Cyre-

næic refugees. As soon as Pheretime heard of this she
went to Egypt and asked Aryandes to aid her in punish-
ing the murderers of her son. Aryandes gladly assented,
and sent an army under the Egyptian Aahmes and a fleet
under the Persian Badres against Barcæa. Pheretime
herself accompanied the army. The combined forces
reached the city without loss, and the extradition of Arkesilaus's murderers was demanded but refused. The city
was hereupon beleaguered, but held out for nine months,
and was then captured only by stratagem. Pheretime's
revenge was terrible: her son's murderers were crucified
and their wives were cruelly mutilated. Part of the prisoners taken were handed over to Pheretime, part were
sent to Persia and settled in Bactria by Darius. The
army now advanced to Euhesperides, but soon began the
retreat. A wrangle between the commanders had led to
this retreat, and soon after they started a messenger came
from Aryandes ordering them home. On the retreat the
Libyans are said to have attacked and cut to pieces the
rear-guard. Aryandes had a definite object in recalling
the army. He had planned the foundation of an independent Egyptian empire. The details of his plan are
unknown, but he seems to have become dangerous, for he
was executed at the command of Darius.

Late in the year 517 B. C. Darius himself came to
Egypt. Shortly before his arrival, the Apis-steer which
had been enthroned in the reign of Cambyses died and
Darius offered a reward of one hundred talents to whom-
soever would find the new Apis. Darius thus returned to
the policy inaugurated by Cambyses when he first came
to Egypt. Early in his reign he ordered Hor-utja-suten-
net to fill the complement of temple scribes. This noble
accordingly established schools for the scribes and fitted
them out with everything that was needful, for Darius
well knew that this was the best way of preserving the
names of the gods, their temples and incomes forever. He
repaired the temple of Memphis and made valuable presents to the temple of Edfu; but his chief work was the
building of the temple in the Oasis El-Kargeh. We see,
thus, that Darius posed everywhere as a pharaoh, and so
successfully did he carry out this policy that he completely won the hearts of his Egyptian subjects in a very short
while.

Like Nekau, Darius determined to re-establish the connection between the Nile and the Red Sea that had existed in the times of Seti I and Ramses II. A stele bearing on one side an inscription in hieroglyphics and on the other side a translation of this in Median, Persian, and Babylonian, recounts this fact. This inscription reads : " I am a Persian. With the aid of Persia I conquered Egypt. I gave orders to dig this canal from the river Nile which flows in Egypt to the sea which is connected with Persia. Then this canal was dug as I had ordered. But I said : ' Now go and destroy half this canal from the city of Bira to the sea, because such is my will.' " Why this last order was given he does not say. Diodorus and Strabo, however, relate that his engineers represented to him that if the canal were completed the Red Sea, which lay higher than Egypt, would flood the country. It is a curious fact that Herodotus regarded the canal as completed, for he says it was four days' journey long, and wide enough to allow two triremes to pass in line. It is further noteworthy that Cambyses had already founded a city, named *Cambyson*, after him, near the route of the canal. Probably he had intended to undertake the work, but had died before it was begun.

The most important act of his reign was that he erected Egypt, together with Libya, Barcæa, and Cyrenæ, into the sixth satrapy. This satrapy had to pay an annual tax of seven hundred talents, or eight hundred and twenty-six thousand dollars. The fisheries of Lake Mœris were declared to be the property of the crown. The Egyptians had to furnish the Persian garrison of the citadel of Memphis one hundred and twenty thousand bushels of grain annually. Further, they had to furnish salt and Nile water for the royal table. The income of the city of Anthylla was given the Queen of Persia, according to some accounts for her shoes, according to others for her belts, or, as we would say, for pin-money.

Late in this reign, four years after the battle of Marathon, the Egyptians made an effort to regain their independence. They made a man named *Chabbash* king ; but before Darius could march against the rebels he died, 485 B. C., in the thirty-sixth year of his reign.

Xerxes (Eg., *Cheshiresh*, 485–472 B. C.).—When Xerxes came to the throne of Persia, *Chabbash* had firmly

established himself in Egypt. He assumed the coronation-name of *Senen-Tanen Setep-en-Ptah*, and was exer-
cising all the functions of a legitimate pharaoh. In the
second year of his reign he interred an Apis, probably the
one that was enthroned in the thirty-first year of Darius's
reign. Several temples, among them that of Buto, were
given large tracts of land. The Egyptian king did not
neglect to prepare to meet an attack from Persia which
could be expected every day. The mouths of the Nile
were strongly fortified, and everything was put in readi-
ness to repel the expected attack. The rebel king could
not, however, hold out against Xerxes. The country was
again subdued, and *Achaemenes*, the king's brother, was
appointed satrap with orders to institute a very strict *ré-
gime*. Achaemenes kept his position all his life, and it
was probably his harsh rule that led to the revolt of Inaros. In the war with Greece the Egyptians had to fit out
and man two hundred vessels, the crews of which were
afterward transferred to the land army and took part in
the battle of Plataea.

Artaxerxes (Eg., *Artachsheshes*) and the Revolt of Inaros (464–448 B. C.).—After the assassina-
tion of Xerxes the country was for a while plunged into
anarchy and divided by wars for the succession, which
were finally brought to a close in 464 B. C. by the accession of Artaxerxes. During these wars the Persians lost
control over several provinces, among which was Egypt.
As they had taken advantage of the temporary weakness
of the Persians after their defeat at Marathon, the Egyptians now took advantage of the anarchy existing in Persia to make another fight for liberty. Cyrenæ had during
the past reign gradually regained its independence, and
the Libyans seem to have been left pretty much to themselves since the revolt of Chabbash; in fact, it would seem
that this rebel was a Libyan or of Libyan descent. His
name certainly is not Egyptian.

At the time Artaxerxes came to the throne, a sover-
eign named *Inaros*, the son of *Psemtek*, ruled over the
Libyan tribes that dwelt on the Egyptian border. This
chief determined to free Egypt from the Persian yoke,
and easily succeeded in inciting the greater part of the
country to revolt. The people chose him king, drove out
the Persian tax-collectors, and raised an army. The first

object of the new pharaoh was to secure allies against Persia. He easily succeeding in getting aid from Cyrenæ. He next turned to Athens, and the Athenians concluded a treaty with him, and ordered their fleet of two hundred sail, which lay at Cyprus, to proceed to Egypt. This fleet forced its way up the Nile as far as Memphis, two thirds of which city had already fallen into the hands of the Egyptians. The citadel, however, was still held by the Persians, and such Egyptians as had remained loyal to Persia. This citadel the combined forces of the Egyptians and Greeks beleaguered, but all attempts to reduce it failed. Meanwhile Artaxerxes, hearing of the revolt, had confirmed his uncle Achæmenes as satrap of Egypt, and sent him an army of three hundred thousand men to put down the rebellion. This army entered the Delta without encountering any opposition. At Papremis they were met by the combined forces of the Egyptians and Athenians and utterly routed. They fled from the field, and the Egyptians pursuing, a terrible massacre ensued ; only a mere fragment of the vast army succeeded in getting safely behind the walls of Memphis (462 B. C.). Achæmenes himself was mortally wounded, and died soon after the battle. His body was sent to Artaxerxes.

The Persian king now began intriguing for the withdrawal of the Athenian troops, offering the Spartans large subsidies if they would attack Athens. Failing in this, he at last fitted out a new army, and placed it under command of Artabanos and Megabyzos, two brave generals. In 461 B. C. this new army of three hundred thousand men marched into Cilicia. Here a halt was made, and the Cilicians and Phœnicians were ordered to equip a fleet. Three hundred triremes having been fitted out, they were manned with the best troops in the army. The land forces were put through a careful course of training. Meanwhile the war had come to a standstill in Egypt. The combined forces of the Egyptians and Athenians still lay before the citadel of Memphis, but could not compel its surrender. At length, in 460 B. C., the Persian army began to move. Marching along the coast so as to keep in constant communication with the fleet, the army at length entered Egypt without having encountered any opposition. The allies seem to have been utterly blind to the threatening danger, deeming it improbable that the

Persians should again attack them after their terrible defeat at Papremis two years before. They were, however,
pretty rudely awakened when they suddenly found themselves face to face with the Persian army. They accepted
the proffered battle and were utterly routed. Memphis
was relieved, and the Athenians withdrew with their ships
to the island of Prosopitis, in the Nile. A year and a half
they held out here, until the Persians dammed the Nile,
and thus beached the Athenian ships. The Athenians
burning their vessels, intrenched themselves and prepared
to sell their lives dearly; but the object of the Persians
was not to destroy them, but to render them useless as
allies of Inaros, and to drive them from Egypt. They
therefore concluded a treaty with the Athenians, guaran-
teeing them a safe retreat. In this manner part of the
Athenian army succeeded in reaching Athens by way of
Libya and Cyrenæ. Inaros was not so fortunate: wounded
and captured in an engagement, he was sent to Persia, his
life being spared. Here, at the instigation of Queen
Amestris, who desired to avenge Achæmenes, he was
crucified and his companions were beheaded.

The war was not, however, ended yet. The Athenians
had sent a fleet of fifty sail to re-enforce their fleet before
Memphis. It entered the Mendesian branch of the Nile,
where it was surprised by the Phœnicians, and almost
completely destroyed, only a few vessels escaping. For
several years *Amyrtæus* (Egyptian, *Amenrut*) succeeded
in holding his own in the Delta. Like his friend and ally
Inaros, he sent to Athens for aid, and sixty ships were
ordered by Cimon to proceed to Egypt from Cyprus; but
these vessels were of no avail, for they returned to Athens
on hearing of Cimon's death .(449 B. C.). In 445 B. C. a
certain *Psemtek* (Greek, *Psammetichos*) seems to have
held an independent position in Egypt, for he sent thirty
thousand bushels of grain to Athens.

After the rebellion had been suppressed, Artabanos and
Megabyzos returned home, and *Larsames* was appointed
satrap. *Thannyras*, the son of *Inaros*, and *Pausiris*,
the son of *Amyrtæus*, were given their hereditary princi-
palities — the former probably Libya and the latter the
western part of the Delta. How long these princes reigned,
and in what relation they stood to Persia, we can not say.
Herodotus, who visited Egypt shortly after the suppression

of the revolt of Inaros, found Egypt tranquil under Persian rule. There was then no trace of an independent Egyptian kingdom, and the only traces of the late troubles were the bleaching bones on the old battle-fields. Egypt was again prosperous and happy, celebrating its old festivals in the old manner—a striking proof of the elasticity of the people.

The reigns of Xerxes II, Sogdianus, and Darius II, had but little import for Egypt (448–414 B. C.), except that in the latter part of Darius's reign the Egyptians again revolted, and this time succeeded in gaining their independence, under the leadership of *Amenrut.*

§ 2. *The Twenty-eighth Dynasty (414–408 B. C.).*

Amenrut (Greek, *Amyrtœos*). — Late in the year 415 B. C. Amenrut, of Sais, succeeded, with the aid of Greek mercenaries, in delivering Egypt from the Persian rule. No details of this successful revolt are known, but it would seem that it stood in some connection with the revolt of *Pissuthnes* in Lydia, which occurred at about the same time, while that of *Amorges* in Caria (413–412 B. C.) kept the Persian kings busy at home, so that Amenrut was enabled to establish himself firmly on the Egyptian throne. The whole of Egypt soon came under his control, and it would even seem that he was able to take the offensive against Persia. A remark of Thucydides appears to point to the fact that he was allied with Athens in 412 and 411 B. C. In 410 B. C., according to Diodorus, he, together with the King of Arabia, threatened the Phœnician seaboard, and the Persian king sent a fleet of three hundred sail against them. Despite these successes, he could not hold himself on the throne, but was deposed by the mercenaries. His son was excluded from the succession, and *Naïf-āa-rut* elevated to the throne (408 B. C.).

§ 3. *The Twenty-ninth Dynasty (408–386 B. C.).*

Naïf-āa-rut I (*Nepherites*) (408–402 B. C.).—The first act of the new king was to appoint his son *Necht-Hor-heb* (Nectanebus) co-regent; but this act did not please the people, and Prince Necht-Hor-heb was banished to his city, from which he returned twenty-one years later as king. All that we know of this king is, that an Apis-steer was buried in the second year of his reign. Some blocks, bearing his name, found at Thebes, prove that he built there.

Pa-sa-mut (Greek, *Psamuthis*) (402–401 B. C.).— According to the Demotic Chronicles, this pharaoh had not served the gods well, and consequently had not been generally recognized. This assertion is not well founded, as the inscriptions prove. Numerous blocks of stone bearing his name, *Rā-oueser-setep-en-Rā Pa-sa-Mut*, found at Thebes, prove that he built at the temple of Amon.

Haker (Greek, *Acoris*) (400–386 B. C.) ruled thir-teen years. He had been, like his predecessor, placed on the throne by the mercenaries, and, as he was just and looked after the decaying temples, he was retained as king as long as he lived. He was busy repairing temples in all parts of Egypt. Diodorus relates that Haker became in-volved in the wars between Greece and Persia. At this time Sparta was at war with the common enemy, and Agesilaos sent envoys to Egypt asking for aid. Haker sent him timber for one hundred triremes and five hundred thousand bushels of grain. These stores were forwarded to Rhodos, which city had meanwhile deserted Sparta and joined Persia, so that the present intended for that state came to be used against it. We hear also, through Theo-pompus, of a treaty of alliance which this king concluded with the Pisidians, but we know not what came of this al-liance. Possibly it stood in some connection with a war between Egypt and Persia that lasted from 390–387 B. C., and in which Isocrates says the three greatest Persian generals—Abrokomas, Tethranes, and Pharnabazos—had fought against Egypt for three years without accomplish-ing anything, just before the beginning of the Cypriote war. This war broke out in 386 B. C., King Euagoras of Cyprus revolting against Persia, and calling on Haker for aid. The pharaoh sent him troops, but before the war was well begun he died (386 B. C.).

Naïf-āa-rut II (Greek, *Nepherites*) (386 B. C.), the son of Haker, succeeded his father on the throne with the aid of the troops; but the people did not support him, and consequently the soldiers deserted him and killed his son. They hereupon "restored the right"—i. e., they placed on the throne *Necht-Hor-heb*, the son of *Naïf-āa-*

rut I, who had been banished and deprived of his right to the succession.

§ 4. *The Thirtieth Dynasty (386–349* B. C.*).*

Necht-Hor-heb (*Nectanebus I*) (386–368 B. C.).— The Egyptian monuments teach us nothing of this king's reign. Diodorus has, however, luckily preserved an account of him which proves that he was the most important Egyptian king of this entire period. In his reign Egypt again took an influential place among the nations of the world ; it could defy Persia, and could dare to assert its influence in Asia. In this reign falls the Cypriote war that began shortly before the death of Haker. The war had dragged along for several years before Artaxerxes saw the need of specially exerting 'himself to put an end to it. He now raised an army of three hundred thousand men, which was put under command of his son-in-law Orontes, and fitted out a fleet of three hundred triremes, the command of which was given to Teribazus. These combined forces proceeded to Cyprus, and at once began to push the war. Euagoras had also made extensive preparations. Necht-Hor-heb sent him a goodly army ; Hecatombos, of Caria, sent money ; several Phœnician cities, among them Tyre, joined him ; the King of Arabia, and other rulers hostile to Persia, sent troops. Thus he managed to get together ninety ships and six thousand native troops, besides the contingents of his allies. His privateers succeeded in cutting off the grain transport for the Persian army, and a mutiny broke out among the troops. Glus, the newly appointed Persian admiral, consequently had to go to Cilicia for grain before undertaking anything. Euagoras received his provisions and large amounts of money from Egypt. He was now enabled to increase his fleet to two hundred sail, fifty ships having been sent him from Egypt. With this fleet he attacked the Persian ships, and, though at first successful, was in the end defeated, after a hotly contested battle. The Persians now began the siege of his capital, Salamis. Though he had won a victory on land shortly before his defeat at sea, Euagoras lost courage, and, after appointing his son Pnytagoras commander in Salamis, he fled from the island. Escorted by ten men-of-war, he went to Egypt

14

to solicit further aid. Necht-Hor-heb gave him a sum of money, somewhat less than he had expected, but sufficient for his present purpose, and so he returned home (383 B. C.). He found the siege of Salamis still going on, and, as his allies were beginning to desert him, he offered his submission. After a long delay the decision came that he should remain King of Cyprus as a Persian vassal, and must pay an annual tribute.)

The war with Egypt continued. Glus, the Persian admiral, revolted shortly after the surrender of Salamis, and, allying himself with Egypt and Sparta, began a new war against Persia. He was, however, assassinated soon after, and thus his plans came to naught. Now that he had brought the war in Cyprus to a successful close, the Persian king determined to punish his inveterate enemy, the King of Egypt. Necht-Hor-heb knew what was coming, and made his preparations accordingly. He began hiring mercenaries, and as he offered high pay and costly presents, he soon had collected a fine army. As general he called Chabrias, of Athens, who accepted the call without first asking the permission of his government, and going to Egypt conducted the preparations for the war with great energy. Pharnabazos, the Persian commander-in-chief, was also very busy with his preparations. He sent envoys to Athens to accuse Chabrias of alienating the good feelings of Persia from Athens, and to ask the Athenians to send him Iphicrates as general. Chabrias was accordingly recalled, and Iphicrates sent to Persia (between 376 and 374 B. C.). At length, 374 B. C., Pharnabazos was ready. He had collected an army of two hundred thousand native troops and twenty thousand Greek mercenaries, three hundred men-of-war, and a large fleet of smaller craft. This force mustered at Akê, and thence proceeded along the coast toward Egypt. Early in the summer they reached the border, after several attempts to betray the army had been detected and prevented by Iphicrates.

Necht-Hor-heb had regular reports concerning the strength and movements of the enemy. His plan of operations was very simple : he relied on the natural bulwarks of the land. All the border forts were greatly strengthened and the mouths of the Nile were strongly fortified, the strongest fortifications being erected on the

Pelusian branch, the one nearest to Asia. When the Persians approached this branch they found it too strong, and determined to attempt some less strongly fortified branch of the river. Consequently they put to sea, and soon after appeared on the Mendesian branch, where they landed three thousand men, who advanced on the fort. An equal number of Egyptians sallied from the fort to meet them; but the enemy being constantly re-enforced from their ships, the Egyptians were almost cut to pieces. A small remnant of their force escaped to the fort, closely pursued by Iphicrates's men, who entered the fort together with them. It fell, its walls were razed, and the inhabitants were sold into slavery. Iphicrates, who had found out from one of the prisoners that Memphis was unprotected, advised an immediate advance on that city. Pharnabazos replied that they had better await the remainder of their army, so as to be sure of taking the town. Iphicrates now proposed to go down with his Greeks and take the city. This made the Persian suspicious, and he refused him permission. This quarrel between the Persian leaders gave Necht-Hor-heb time to collect an army at Memphis and to move with all his force against the Persians in the Delta. Several combats took place, in which the Egyptians were mostly successful, but no decisive battle was fought. Meanwhile the Nile rose, and soon the entire Delta was converted into a vast lake. Hereupon the Persians, despairing of success, returned to Asia. Iphicrates, who feared violence on account of his quarrel with Pharnabazos, went straight to Athens. For several years the army lay in Asia ready to renew the war at any time, and in 372 B. C. Timotheos went to Asia to offer his services to the Persian king. Nothing was done, however, and the great campaign against Egypt, so pompously begun, proved in the end a dismal failure.

Despite the fact that he was almost constantly at war, this pharaoh carefully kept the temples in repair. He built at Edfu, Karnak, Medinet Habu, Abydos, Bubastis, Memphis, and other places. After a busy and eventful reign of eighteen years he died.

Teher (Greek, *Tachos*, 368–361 B C.).—It would seem that after the death of Necht-Hor-heb, troubles regarding the succession broke out. The list of Manetho gives Tachos (i. e., Teher) only two years and Nectanebus II (Necht-nebef) eighteen years, while the accounts given by the Greek authors go to prove that Tachos still reigned in 361 B. C. It would seem, then, that Teher had appointed Necht-nebef co-regent in 367 B. C., and that this latter monarch had, in imitation of the older pharaohs, dated his accession to the throne from the time he was made co-regent. According to the Demotic Chronicles, Teher was the son of Necht-Hor-heb ; according to the Greek authors, he was that monarch's cousin. The Egyptian inscriptions tell us nothing of this king, and from the Greek historians we know only the events of the closing year of his reign,

In 361 B. C. a great revolt against Persia broke out in Asia, and Teher naturally assisted the rebels. He collected a large army and fitted out a strong fleet. He also hired great numbers of mercenaries in Greece and made a treaty of alliance with Sparta. The strength of the coalition thus formed against Persia would have been sufficient for its purpose had it not been weakened by treachery; Orontes, the commander-in-chief of the Asiatic rebels, was the first to prove a traitor, and soon after Rheomithres, who had received the aid furnished by Teher, five hundred talents (twenty-eight thousand five hundred pounds) of silver and fifty men-of war, followed his example. Notwithstanding this defection the forces at the command of the pharaoh were quite strong, consisting of two hundred splendidly equipped men-of-war, eighty thousand native troops, and ten thousand choice Greek mercenaries. The command of the mercenaries devolved on King Agesilaos of Sparta, who had come over with one thousand hoplites. The Athenian Chabrias was given command of the fleet, while Teher himself retained command of the native troops. Chabrias was the special favorite of the pharaoh, who is said even to have gone so far at his advice as to levy a tax on the temple estates and on the exports and imports of the country while the war lasted. Agesilaos was less regarded. His coming had been looked forward to with considerable expectation. Preparations had been made for a grand reception, and valuable presents had been ordered. When he did come he proved quite a disappointment. His small stature and extreme plainness awakened the scorn of the Egyptians, and a number of jokes were circulated at his expense. This naturally enraged him, and, though he did his full duty by Teber, there was a coolness between the two kings which was still further augmented by the fact that Teher, disregarding the advice of the Spartan, proceeded to conduct the war on his own plan.

Agesilaos had advised Teher to await the Persians in Egypt, but the pharaoh was determined to take the offensive and invade Syria. Phœnicia fell an easy prey to his attack, and the king sent his cousin and co-regent, Necht-nebef, to take the cities of Syria. These movements were successful, and matters were assuming the most hopeful aspect, when *Teher,* the general whom the pharaoh had appointed regent of Egypt for the time of his absence, revolted and offered the crown to Necht-nebef. The latter assented, and soon had won over the army and its officers and all the people of Egypt. All he needed now was the support of the Greek mercenaries. Accordingly, he sent envoys to Agesilaos and Chabrias soliciting their support. Agesilaos despatched messengers to Sparta asking how he should act, and, receiving the reply that he should do what he deemed most advantageous for Sparta, he declared for Necht-nebef. Chabrias, who had at first determined to remain loyal to Teher, seeing his colleague desert that monarch, and being unable to help him alone, followed Agesilaos's example. He left Egypt, however, soon after, never to return. Teher fled first to Sidon and thence to Artaxerxes, who not only forgave him his former enmity, but even made him commander-in-chief of the army that was preparing to invade Egypt. For a while he lived at the Persian court, where he spent his time in wild orgies until he finally died of dysentery. The command of the Persian army he never actually took. This pharaoh reigned two years alone, and six years in conjunction with Necht-nebef.

Necht-nebef (Greek, *Nectanebus II,* 361–349 B. C.).—In 361 B. C. the last native pharaoh ascended the Egyptian throne. The first act of his reign was to give up the conquests in Phœnicia and Syria and to withdraw within the boundaries of Egypt. The reason for this step was most probably that the internal dissensions had not yet come to a close. A Mendesian had appeared as a pretender to the crown, and had succeeded in gaining a large following and raising an army. He even attempted to gain over King Agesilaos, but he remained loyal to his ally. Necht-nebef, carefully avoiding a battle, retired to a fortified town, where his rival beleaguered him. Already the besieged were beginning to lose heart, as their provisions gave out, when Agesilaos saved them. Sallying from the town, he broke the ranks of the besiegers and drew up his troops in the plain so that both flanks rested on canals. In the battle that ensued the bravery of the Greeks prevailed over the superior numbers of the Egyptians. The latter were completely routed, the greater part of their number being slain and the rest flying from the field in wild disorder. Necht-nebef was now undisputed ruler of Egypt. Shortly after this victory Agesilaos determined to return home. The grateful king loaded him with presents —according to some authorities he gave him two hundred and thirty talents, or about two hundred and seventy-one thousand four hundred dollars — which he distributed among his troops. On his way to Cyrenæ he died. His body was embalmed and sent to Sparta, where it was buried with royal honors (360 B. C.).

Meanwhile the Persians had completed their preparations, and Artaxerxes had appointed his son, *Ochus*, coregent. Ochus set out for Egypt, but, on hearing the news of his father's death, in 359 B. C., he returned home. Some time later Ochus attempted the subjugation of Egypt, but was defeated by Necht-nebef, who was assisted by two excellent generals, Diophantes of Athens and Lamius of Sparta. This success of the Egyptians encouraged the Phœnicians and the King of Cyprus to strike a blow for independence. They concluded treaties with Necht-nebef and at once began extensive preparations. At the head of the Phœnician towns stood Sidon, which soon succeeded in collecting a large army and vast amounts of military stores. Ochus had, however, not been idle. He had collected an army of three hundred thousand infantry and thirty thousand cavalry, and had fitted out three hundred triremes and five hundred transports. Then he started from Babylon. Before his arrival two of his satraps, Belesys of Syria and Mazaeos of Cilicia, had in vain attempted the reconquest of Phœnicia. They were defeated and driven out of the country by *Tennes*, the King of Sidon, assisted by four thousand Greeks under Mentor, who had been sent him by Necht-nebef. Now came the news that Ochus was approaching, and Tennes lost courage. He sent a trusty messenger to Ochus, asking pardon for his revolt, and offering to aid the king against Egypt. Ochus gladly promised full pardon, even giving him costly presents, and after some hesitation pledged himself to this course. We shall presently see how he kept his word. Ochus had, while advancing on Sidon, despatched envoys to Greece asking the larger states to join in the campaign against Egypt. Athens and Sparta remained neutral. Thebes sent one thousand hoplites under Lacrates, and Argos, three thousand men under Nicostratus, whom Ochus had asked them to send him. The Greek cities of Asia Minor furnished in all six thousand men, making the total number of Greeks in the Persian army aggregate ten thousand men. Ochus now laid siege to Sidon, which was very strongly fortified, and would never have yielded had it not been for the treachery of its king. Tennes persuaded Mentor to join him, and together they succeeded in admitting the Persians into the city. When the Sidonians saw they were lost they destroyed their fleet, locked themselves up in their houses, and set fire to the city. Over forty thousand people are said to have perished in the flames. This so enraged Ochus that he had Tennes put to death. Mentor and his four thousand joined the Persian army. The fall of Sidon was disastrous to the allies, for all of the Phœnician cities, on hearing of the dire news, surrendered at discretion.

About the same time Cyprus again fell into the hands of the Persians. A detachment of eight thousand Greeks, supported by forty triremes, under command of the Athenian Phocion and ex-King Euagoras of Cyprus, succeeded in subduing the island very quickly. Salamis alone held out. Euagoras strained every nerve to capture the city, as he hoped to be made king again. Charges were, however, preferred against him, and consequently Pnytagoras was allowed to keep the city as a vassal of Persia.

The Persians now attacked Egypt. After having suffered severe losses in the desert, they at length reached Pelusium. The Persian troops were drawn up at some distance from the strongly fortified town, while the Greeks camped almost under its walls. The city was garrisoned by five thousand men under Philophron. The first attack was made by the Thebans, who waded the narrow canal

that separated them from the town, and began a battle
which lasted far into the night, but was indecisive. The
forces of Necht-nebef were much inferior to those of the
Persians, consisting of twenty thousand Greeks, twenty
thousand Libyans, and sixty thousand Egyptians; but he
possessed large numbers of river-boats, which could be
used to great advantage in any combat on the Nile; and,
moreover, he had erected a string of strong forts along
the eastern bank of the Pelusic branch. He lacked, however, a good general. Proud of his previous victories over
the Persians, he had neglected to send to Greece for a
general. This mistake proved fatal. He had posted half
his force in the forts, and with the rest he opposed the
advance of the enemy. Before a decisive battle was
fought, Nicostratus succeeded in moving his men to a
point of vantage betrayed to him by an Egyptian, and
strongly intrenched himself. Seeing this, Clinias of Cos,
who was posted near by with seven thousand men, attempted to dislodge him. The attack was repulsed;
Clinias and five thousand of his men fell. This battle was
by no means decisive; but now the want of a good general showed itself in the Egyptian army. Instead of sending a stronger force against Nicostratus, Necht-nebef,
fearing that the Persians would all cross the Nile as easily
as that commander had, lost courage, and, deserting his
forts, retreated to Memphis. Meanwhile, Pelusium was
being besieged by Lacrates, but it made a desperate resistance for several days; when the garrison heard of the
pharaoh's retreat, however, they offered to capitulate. Lacrates promised the Greek troops a safe retreat; and
though Bagoas, who commanded the Persian division of
this corps, attempted to attack them, he was prevented
from doing so by his colleague. Mentor now marched
through the Delta, promising immunity to all who would
surrender at discretion, and threatening all who should re-
sist with the fate of Sidon. Consequently, the Greek and
Egyptian garrisons vied with one another in the rapidity
of their surrenders. Among others, the strong and important fortress of Bubastis surrendered at discretion, and
all the other fortresses of the Delta followed its example.
When Necht-nebef heard of these losses, he dared not
give battle, but, taking the greater part of the moneys in
the state coffers, he fled to Aethiopia. Thus, about 349

B. C., Egypt, after an independence of sixty-five years, again fell into the hands of the Persians, and from this time forth it was destined to be governed by foreign rulers.

§ 5. *The Thirty-first Dynasty, and the Invasion of Alexander (349–331* B. C.).

Of the last three Persian kings not one was of special importance for Egypt. Ochus was a cruel tyrant, whose acts reminded of the times of the insanity of Cambyses. The Greek authors relate stories of his outrages against the Egyptian religion that accord well with what we know of his character. They recount that the people had once on a time nicknamed him "*Onos,*" the ass, and now he determined to have his revenge. The sacred Apis-steer was butchered and eaten by the king and his friends, and an ass was elevated to the position of sacred animal in his stead. The sacred ram of Mendes was likewise slaughtered at the king's command. The walls of the principal cities were razed; the temples were plundered, and their treasures of gold and silver carried off to Persia. Not content with plundering the temples, Ochus stole the sacred writings from the sanctuaries, and compelled the priests to repurchase them at exorbitant prices. As satrap he appointed a Persian named Pherendates, and then he returned home to Babylon loaded with rich booty. Twelve years after the conquest of Egypt Ochus was murdered by Bagoas, who placed the king's son *Arses* on the throne, but he ruled only three years, falling a victim to the same treacherous eunuch that had murdered his father (334 B. C.). In the place of his last victim Bagoas elevated a distant relative of the royal family—his friend Darius—to the throne, and at his hands finally met his merited reward. The king detected the eunuch's plan against his life, and compelled the fellow to swallow the draught intended for himself. Darius III did not long retain the throne he owed to his friend's crime. The Greek invasion, under Alexander's leadership, soon deprived him of his crown. Egypt remained tranquil, almost an uninterested spectator, during the dread struggle between Greece and Persia, even though all of the Persian garrisons had been withdrawn. In the battle of Issus the Egyptian contingent fought with the Persians under its

satrap Sabaces. Their leader fell, and the troops fled
with Darius. In Egypt Mazaces succeeded Sabaces as
satrap, but he had no troops to support his authority. The
power of Persia was crushed, but Egypt did not strike the
one blow that would have sufficed to regain its freedom.
They had, however, sufficient spirit left to defend their
homes against robbers. After the defeat of the Persians
at Issus, Amytas, a Macedonian exile, who had joined
Darius, fled to Tripolis in Phœnicia, collected a fleet and
sailed to Cyprus, where he increased his land-forces.
Thence he sailed to Pelusium, effected a landing, and declared he was the new satrap appointed by Darius. He
then marched through the Delta to Memphis, near which
city he defeated a body of Egyptians. After the victory
his bands dispersed to plunder the rich country seats lying
about the city. While engaged in this work they were
surprised and cut to pieces by the citizens; Amytas fell,
and not a man of his bands escaped.

After taking Tyre and Gaza, Alexander determined
to secure Egypt. He reached Pelusium after a seven
days' march without encountering any resistance. His
fleet awaited him in the harbor. Mazaces, having no
troops, and having no hope of assistance from his unfortunate monarch, had no recourse but surrender. Alexander garrisoned Pelusium and sent the fleet up the Nile
to Memphis. With the army he marched along the river-
bank to Heliopolis, and crossing the river at this point
soon entered Memphis. The great king entered the ancient capital, not in the character of a conqueror, but like
a pharaoh of old, observing all the old religious ceremonies. He offered sacrifices to the gods, and instituted
athletic games and prize contests in the fine arts in which
celebrated Greek masters took part. The Egyptians were
naturally captivated by this conduct, which was so different from that of the last Persian rulers, and it is not at all
surprising that a mystic romance was soon woven about
the person of the Macedonian king. According to this
romance, Necht-nebef had not fled to Aethiopia, but to
Macedonia. He was a great magician, and as such he
took the form of Jupiter-Amon, and in this form approached Queen Olympias, the wife of King Philip. Alexander was thus, the story continues, the son of Necht-
nebef, and not of Philip. The romance thus made Alex-

ander the legitimate heir of the old pharaohs, and the avenger of his father Necht-nebef. It would seem that Alexander rather favored the spread of this legend, as he knew it would greatly strengthen his hold on the Egyptian people. Sailing down the Nile from Memphis through the Canopic branch, he went to sea from Canopus. Landing at the outlet of Lake Maroetis, near the ancient town of *Rakoté*, he saw at a glance that the place offered unequaled harbor facilities. He therefore determined to found a city here which should bear his name; and thus was founded the city of Alexandria, the most important and most permanent of the many towns founded by this king. This city soon became the great intellectual exchange between the nations of the Occident and the Orient, the mother of a new civilization. Here European and Oriental philosophy, religion, and science met on a footing of equality, and views were exchanged and new systems inaugurated that completely revolutionized ideas. The philosophy of Philo and the astronomical system of Ptolemy were among the brilliant results of the new civilization. A new art, the Hellenistic, resulted from the interchange of Greek and Oriental—more especially Egyptian—ideas on art. Doubtless, too, the spread of Christianity was much fostered by the cosmopolitan spirit in regard to religious matters which emanated from this city.

From Alexandria the king pushed westward to the famous oasis of Amon. With the assistance of the gods he reached it in safety; the story goes that when the water supply gave out rain fell and that messengers of the god in the shape of ravens conducted the army to the oasis. On the way he was met by a deputation from Cyrenae which offered him a golden crown and costly presents. The city evidently apprehended an attack, and thought it advisable to submit peaceably. As Alexander entered the temple of Amon on the oasis, the high priest hailed him as son of the god. Not knowing that it was customary to designate the pharaohs as sons of Rā and of Amon, the king laid great stress on this greeting. After having made the temple rich presents, Alexander returned to Memphis in safety. Here he instituted a great festival in honor of Jupiter. He now turned his attention to the reorganization of the Egyptian government. The civil government was put into the hands of two Egyptian nomarchoi named *Doloaspis* and *Petisis*, and on the resignation of the former the control of civil matters was intrusted to the latter alone. The commanders of the garrisons and of the various troops of mercenaries, as well as the heads of the commissary departments, were Greeks. Leaving a p   of his army in Egypt, Alexander, early in 331 B.C., leftathe country, never to return. He had so delicately adjusted the government that the various officials effectively held one another in check, and there \could be no chance of a revolt. After Alexander's death his body was brought to Alexandria for interment.

With the conquest of Egypt by Alexander the history of the country comes to a close. The Ptolemies who, after the great king's death, again made Egypt independent, were a Greek family, and the civilization of their times differed materially from that of the older epochs. Under them the old religious traditions were fostered, it is true. but they no longer possessed any vitality—there was no longer a *national* religion as of old. The old religion and language were known to the priests alone, and with every generation they became less and less intelligible even to this class of—well, let us call them official custodians of the ancient traditions, until, with the coming of Christianity in the first century A. D., the old religion gradually passed away. · The Ptolemies themselves were Greeks ; their capital, Alexandria, was a Greek city ; the civilization of their epoch was partly Greek, partly Egyptian. The history of Egypt after the conquest forms an integral part, first of Greek, then of Roman, and, lastly, of Mohammedan history.

CHRONOLOGICAL TABLE.

Mena unites Upper and Lower Egypt,	Not later than	3200 B. C.
Snefru, the founder of the fourth dynasty,	" "	2830 "
Accession of Meri Rā Pepī,	" "	2530 "
Transition Period,	About	2400–2250 "
Accession of Amenemhāt I,	"	2130 '
Usertesen III,	"	2013–1987 "
Amenemhāt III,	"	1986–1942 "
Hyksòs Domination,	"	1780–1530 "
Accession of Aahmes I,		1530 '
Thutmosis III,	"	1480–1427 "
Chuenaten,	"	1376–1364 "
Accession of Horemheb,		1340
Seti I,	"	1316–1289 "
Ramses II,	"	1288–1221 "
Ramses III,	"	1180–1148 "
Accession of Herīhor, the first Priest-King,		1050
Sheshenq I,	"	945–924 "
Pianchi's Invasion,		800
Accession of Shabaka,		728
First Assyrian Invasion,		672
Second Assyrian Invasion,		667
Tanuat Amon's Invasion,		664
Third Assyrian Invasion,		662
Psemtek I,		645–610 "
Nekau,		610–594 "
Battle of Karkemish,		604 '
Nebuchadnezzar invades Egypt,		567
Conquest of Egypt by Cambyses,		525
Revolt of Chabbash,		486 "
Revolt of Inaros,		464–460 "
Amenrut frees Egypt from Persia,		414 "
Necht-Hor-heb,		386–368 "
Necht-nebef,		361–349 "
Conquest of Egypt by Ochus,		349
Conquest of Egypt by Alexander,		331 '

THE END.